Slow Cooker

VOLUME 1

RDA ENTHUSIAST BRANDS, LLC
MILWAUKEE, WI

Taste of Home · Reader's digest

A TASTE OF HOME/READER'S DIGEST BOOK
©2015 RDA Enthusiast Brands, LLC, 1610 N. 2nd St., Suite 102, Milwaukee WI 53212. All rights reserved.
Taste of Home and Reader's Digest are registered trademarks of The Reader's Digest Association, Inc.

EDITORIAL
Editor-in-Chief: Catherine Cassidy
Creative Director: Howard Greenberg
Editorial Operations Director: Kerri Balliet

Managing Editor, Print & Digital Books: Mark Hagen
Associate Creative Director: Edwin Robles Jr.

Editor: Michelle Rozumalski
Associate Editor: Molly Jasinski
Contributing Layout Designer: Jennifer Lynn Ruetz
Editorial Production Manager: Dena Ahlers
Copy Chief: Deb Warlaumont Mulvey
Copy Editors: Dulcie Shoener, Joanne Weintraub
Contributing Copy Editor: Steph Kilen
Content Operations Assistant: Shannon Stroud
Editorial Services Administrator: Marie Brannon

Food Editors: James Schend; Peggy Woodward, RD
Recipe Editors: Mary King; Jenni Sharp, RD; Irene Yeh

Test Kitchen & Food Styling Manager: Sarah Thompson
Test Cooks: Nicholas Iverson (lead), Matthew Hass, Lauren Knoelke
Food Stylists: Kathryn Conrad (senior), Leah Rekau, Shannon Roum
Prep Cooks: Megumi Garcia, Melissa Hansen, Bethany Van Jacobson, Sara Wirtz

Photography Director: Stephanie Marchese
Photographers: Dan Roberts, Jim Wieland
Photographer/Set Stylist: Grace Natoli Sheldon
Set Stylists: Stacey Genaw, Melissa Haberman, Dee Dee Jacq
Photo Studio Assistant: Ester Robards

Editorial Business Manager: Kristy Martin
Editorial Business Associate: Samantha Lea Stoeger

BUSINESS
Vice President, Group Publisher: Kirsten Marchioli
Publisher: Donna Lindskog
General Manager, Taste of Home Cooking School: Erin Puariea
Executive Producer, Taste of Home Online Cooking School: Karen Berner

THE READER'S DIGEST ASSOCIATION, INC.
President and Chief Executive Officer: Bonnie Kintzer
Vice President, Chief Operating Officer, North America: Howard Halligan
Chief Revenue Officer: Richard Sutton
Chief Marketing Officer: Leslie Dukker Doty
Vice President, Content Marketing & Operations: Diane Dragan
Senior Vice President, Global HR & Communications: Phyllis E. Gebhardt, SPHR
Vice President, Brand Marketing: Beth Gorry
Vice President, Chief Technology Officer: Aneel Tejwaney
Vice President, Consumer Marketing Planning: Jim Woods

For other Taste of Home books and products, visit us at **tasteofhome.com.**

For more Reader's Digest products and information, visit **rd.com** (in the United States) or **rd.ca** (in Canada).

International Standard Book Number: 978-1-61765-487-9
Library of Congress Control Number: 2015937792
Component Number: 116000217H

Cover Photography: Taste of Home Photo Studio

Pictured on front cover:
Sausage Pasta Stew, page 237

Pictured on back cover:
Butterscotch-Pecan Bread Pudding, page 225
Sweet-and-Sour Chicken, page 128

EZ-READ is a trademark of RDA Enthusiast Brands, LLC.

Printed in China.
1 3 5 7 9 10 8 6 4 2

BBQ CHICKEN SLIDERS, 94

SLOW-COOKED SPAGHETTI
& MEATBALLS, 119

LOADED MASHED
POTATOES, 30

BUTTERSCOTCH-PECAN
BREAD PUDDING, 225

CONTENTS

LIKE US
facebook.com/tasteofhome

TWEET US
@tasteofhome

FOLLOW US
pinterest.com/taste_of_home

SHOP WITH US
shoptasteofhome.com

SHARE A RECIPE
tasteofhome.com/submit

GARLIC-SESAME
BEEF, 120

Come Home to a Hot, Hearty Favorite!

Brimming with **comfort** and **convenience,** slow cookers are as popular as ever with **today's home cooks.** Make the most of this essential kitchen appliance with the sensational recipes inside **Taste of Home Slow Cooker!**

This can't-miss cookbook features **112 mouthwatering yet easy** favorites, from **best-loved classics** to **exciting new dishes** everyone will crave. Enjoy **savory main** **courses**, standout sides, party appetizers, hearty soups and stews, **luscious desserts** and satisfying breakfasts—even **an entire chapter of lightened-up recipes!**

VERY VANILLA SLOW
COOKER CHEESECAKE, 209

Look for these handy icons for effortless meal planning:

FREEZE IT

Freeze these slow-cooked dishes to enjoy on your busiest days.

POTLUCK

Wow 'em with a crowd-size specialty straight from the slow cooker.

Shared by **home cooks like you** and approved in the *Taste of Home* **Test Kitchen**, these slow-cooked specialties are sure to turn out perfect every time. Dozens of **kitchen hints, two helpful icons** and a **photo of every recipe** make it even simpler to **serve up fantastic fare.**

Featuring **large print** for easy reading, **Taste of Home Slow Cooker** will quickly become your **go-to resource in the kitchen.** In no time at all, you'll be simmering up a scrumptious winner and **new family favorite!**

APPLE-CINNAMON
PORK LOIN, 154

Hot Crab Dip, p. 21

CHAPTER 1

APPETIZERS & BEVERAGES

Snack and sip anytime with these slow-cooked sensations.

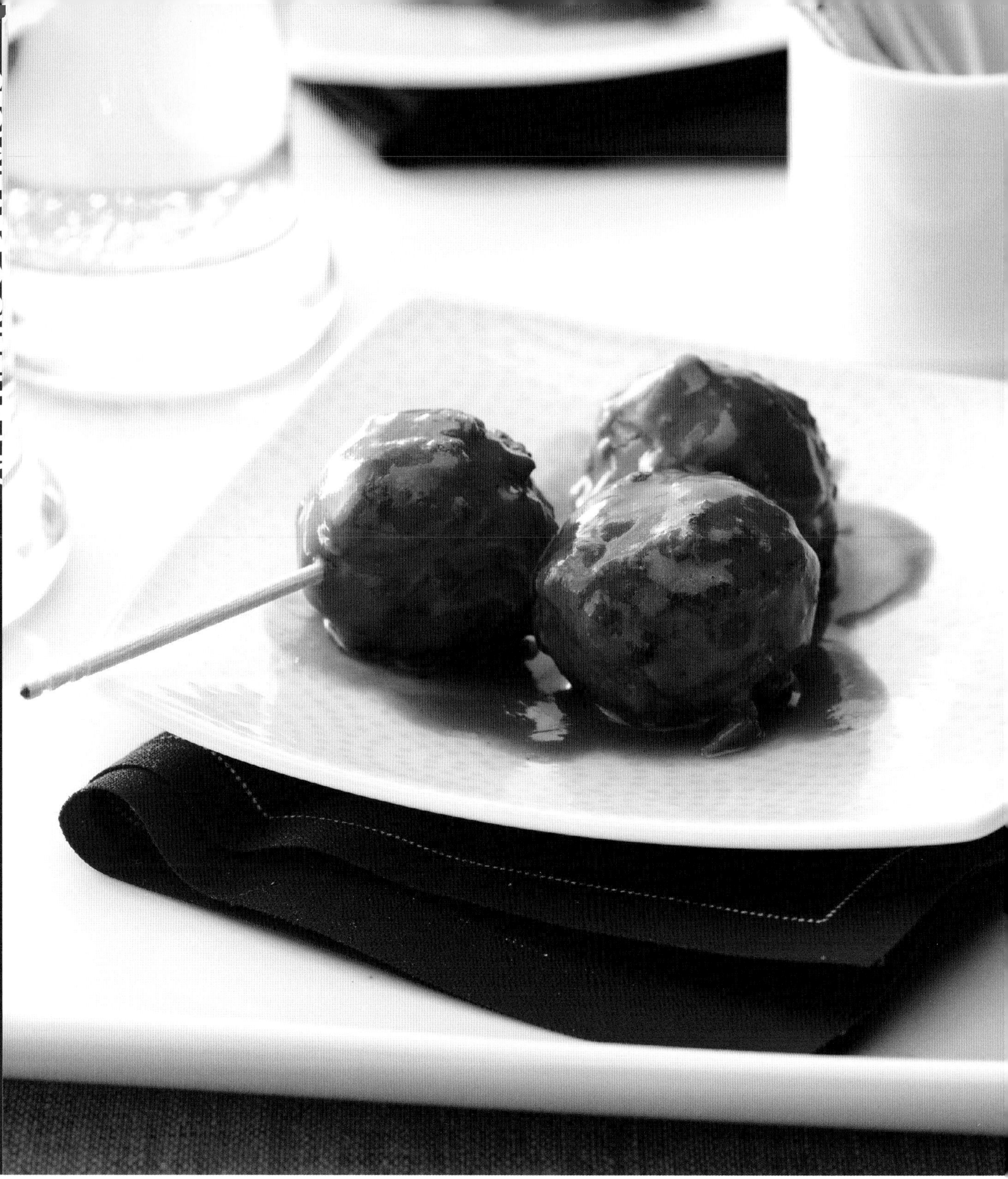

Creamy Cranberry Meatballs

Dress up frozen Swedish meatballs with just four ordinary ingredients—cranberry sauce, gravy mix, Dijon mustard and whipping cream. My guests can't get enough!

—AMY WARREN MAINEVILLE, OH

PREP: 10 MIN. • **COOK:** 3 HOURS
MAKES: ABOUT 5 DOZEN

- 2 envelopes brown gravy mix
- 1 package (32 ounces) frozen fully cooked Swedish meatballs
- 2/3 cup jellied cranberry sauce
- 2 teaspoons Dijon mustard
- 1/4 cup heavy whipping cream

Prepare the gravy mix according to package directions. In a 4-qt. slow cooker, combine the meatballs, cranberry sauce, Dijon mustard and gravy. Cover and cook on low for 3-4 hours or until heated through, adding cream during the last 30 minutes of cooking.

TOP TIP

Have leftovers of this rich and saucy appetizer? Then you have a head start on a delicious dinner tomorrow! Simply store the extras in the refrigerator, reheat them on the stove and serve over a bed of hot cooked egg noodles, rice or instant mashed potatoes. Round out the meal with a quick side salad.

Sweet & Spicy Chicken Wings

Hot from the slow cooker, the meat literally falls off the bones of these flavorful wings. Spice lovers will definitely get a kick out of the generous sprinkling of red pepper flakes.

—SUE BAYLESS PRIOR LAKE, MN

PREP: 25 MIN. • **COOK:** 5 HOURS
MAKES: ABOUT 2½ DOZEN

---

3   pounds chicken wings
1½ cups ketchup
1   cup packed brown sugar
1   small onion, finely chopped
¼   cup finely chopped sweet red pepper
2   tablespoons chili powder
2   tablespoons Worcestershire sauce
1½ teaspoons crushed red pepper flakes
1   teaspoon ground mustard
1   teaspoon dried basil
1   teaspoon dried thyme
1   teaspoon pepper

Cut wings into three sections; discard wing tip sections. Place the chicken in a 4-qt. slow cooker. In a small bowl, combine the remaining ingredients. Pour over chicken; stir until coated. Cover and cook on low for 5-6 hours or until chicken juices run clear.

NOTE Uncooked chicken wing sections (wingettes) may be substituted for whole chicken wings.

Slow Cooker Candied Nuts

Sugar, spice and everything nice make a can't-stop-munching mix of coated pecans, walnuts and almonds. I give brimming jars as gifts to family and friends at Christmastime.
—YVONNE STARLIN HERMITAGE, TN

PREP: 10 MIN. • **COOK:** 2 HOURS
MAKES: 4 CUPS

½ cup butter, melted
½ cup confectioners' sugar
1½ teaspoons ground cinnamon
¼ teaspoon ground ginger
¼ teaspoon ground allspice
1½ cups pecan halves
1½ cups walnut halves
1 cup unblanched almonds

1. In a greased 3-qt. slow cooker, mix the melted butter, confectioners' sugar and spices. Add the nuts; toss to coat. Cook, covered, on low 2-3 hours or until nuts are crisp, stirring once.

2. Transfer the nuts to waxed paper to cool completely. Store in an airtight container.

TOP TIP

Store your ground spices in tightly closed glass containers or heavy-duty plastic containers in a cool, dry place. Avoid storing them in direct sunlight, over the stove or near other heat sources. For best flavor, keep ground spices for up to 6 months. They can be used if they are older, but the flavor may not be as intense.

POTLUCK

Five-Cheese Spinach & Artichoke Dip

Whenever I'm invited to an event, this rich appetizer is invited, too. I get requests to bring it to weddings, holiday gatherings, parties—you name it. Pair the cheesy dip with your favorite crackers or bread chips.

—**NOELLE MYERS** GRAND FORKS, ND

PREP: 20 MIN. • **COOK:** 2½ HOURS
MAKES: 16 SERVINGS (¼ CUP EACH)

1   jar (12 ounces) roasted sweet red peppers
1   jar (6½ ounces) marinated quartered artichoke hearts
1   package (10 ounces) frozen chopped spinach, thawed and squeezed dry
8   ounces fresh mozzarella cheese, cubed
1½ cups (6 ounces) shredded Asiago cheese
2   packages (3 ounces each) cream cheese, softened and cubed
1   cup (4 ounces) crumbled feta cheese
⅓   cup shredded provolone cheese
⅓   cup minced fresh basil
¼   cup finely chopped red onion
2   tablespoons mayonnaise
2   garlic cloves, minced
     Assorted crackers

1. Drain the roasted sweet red peppers, reserving 1 tablespoon liquid; chop the peppers. Drain the artichokes, reserving 2 tablespoons liquid; coarsely chop the artichokes.

2. In a 3-qt. slow cooker coated with cooking spray, combine the spinach, cheeses, basil, onion, mayonnaise, garlic, artichoke hearts and peppers. Stir in the reserved pepper and artichoke liquids. Cook, covered, on high 2 hours. Stir dip; cook, covered, 30-60 minutes longer. Stir before serving; serve with crackers.

TOP TIP

Compared to most commercially produced mozzarella cheese, fresh mozzarella is soft and moist. Featuring a mild, delicate and somewhat milky flavor, fresh mozzarella is usually shaped into balls and stored in brine. After purchase, it should be refrigerated in the brine and eaten within a few days.

Cheesy Pizza Fondue

I always keep the ingredients for my pizza fondue on hand for spur-of-the-moment gatherings. Everyone likes dipping chewy cubes of Italian bread into the savory sauce.
—**NEL CARVER** MOSCOW, ID

PREP: 10 MIN. • **COOK:** 4 HOURS
MAKES: 4 CUPS

- 1 jar (29 ounces) meatless spaghetti sauce
- 2 cups (8 ounces) shredded part-skim mozzarella cheese
- 1/4 cup shredded Parmesan cheese
- 2 teaspoons dried oregano
- 1 teaspoon dried minced onion
- 1/4 teaspoon garlic powder
  Cubed Italian bread

1. In a 1½-qt. slow cooker, combine the spaghetti sauce, cheeses, oregano, onion and garlic powder.

2. Cover and cook on low for 4-6 hours or until heated through and cheese is melted. Serve with bread.

TOP TIP

Make sure to choose a slow cooker that is the appropriate size for the amount of food you're making. For example, to serve just a small amount of dip or fondue, smaller slow cookers are ideal. A slow cooker should be from half to two-thirds full.

Slow Cooker Caramel Apple Cider

Love caramel apples? Sip this indulgent cider topped with whipped cream. It's a heartwarming treat on a chilly day.
—*TASTE OF HOME* **TEST KITCHEN**

PREP: 5 MIN. • **COOK:** 2 HOURS
MAKES: 12 SERVINGS (¾ CUP EACH)

- 8 cups apple cider or juice
- 1 cup caramel flavoring syrup
- ¼ cup lemon juice
- 1 vanilla bean
- 2 cinnamon sticks (3 inches)
- 1 tablespoon whole allspice
  Whipped cream, hot caramel ice cream topping and cinnamon sticks (3 inches), optional

1. In a 3-qt. slow cooker, combine the apple cider, caramel syrup and lemon juice. Split vanilla bean and scrape seeds; add the seeds to cider mixture. Place the bean, cinnamon sticks and allspice on a double thickness of cheesecloth; bring up corners of cloth and tie with string to form a bag. Add to cider mixture.

2. Cover and cook on low for 2-3 hours or until heated through. Discard the spice bag. Pour cider into mugs; garnish with whipped cream, caramel topping and additional cinnamon sticks if desired.

NOTE This recipe was tested with Torani brand flavoring syrup. Look for it in the coffee section.

Hot Crab Dip

I have a big family, work full-time and coach soccer and football. So I really appreciate recipes that are simple to fix. This creamy crab dip takes only five minutes to get into the slow cooker. Cooking just doesn't get much easier than that!

—TERI RASEY CADILLAC, MI

PREP: 5 MIN. • **COOK:** 3 HOURS
MAKES: ABOUT 5 CUPS

½ cup milk
⅓ cup salsa
3 packages (8 ounces each) cream cheese, cubed
2 packages (8 ounces each) imitation crabmeat, flaked
1 cup thinly sliced green onions
1 can (4 ounces) chopped green chilies
   Assorted crackers

In a small bowl, combine the milk and salsa. Transfer to a greased 3-qt. slow cooker. Stir in cream cheese, crab, onions and chilies. Cover and cook on low for 3-4 hours, stirring every 30 minutes. Serve with crackers.

TOP TIP

Is your favorite party dip baked in the oven? Try assembling the dip ahead of time and then heating it in your slow cooker instead. It'll free up your oven for any other baked dishes you may like to make, and you can keep the dip warm for guests during the party by serving directly from the slow cooker.

Championship Bean Dip

When I arrive at a party or other get-together, I inevitably hear, "You brought your bean dip, didn't you?" If we're lucky enough to have leftovers, we take full advantage by using them to make delicious burritos for lunch or dinner the next day. I must have given out this recipe a hundred times.

—WENDI WAVRIN LAW OMAHA, NE

PREP: 10 MIN. • **COOK:** 2 HOURS
MAKES: 4½ CUPS

- 1 can (16 ounces) refried beans
- 1 cup picante sauce
- 1 cup (4 ounces) shredded Monterey Jack cheese
- 1 cup (4 ounces) shredded cheddar cheese
- ¾ cup sour cream
- 1 package (3 ounces) cream cheese, softened
- 1 tablespoon chili powder
- ¼ teaspoon ground cumin
  Tortilla chips and salsa

In a large bowl, combine the first eight ingredients; transfer to a 1½-qt. slow cooker. Cover and cook on high for 2 hours or until heated through, stirring once or twice. Serve with tortilla chips and salsa.

TOP TIP

Want tasty ideas for using up leftover tortilla chips from a party? Finely crush the chips and use them in place of dry bread crumbs as a coating for poultry or fish. Or sprinkle coarsely crushed chips on spicy soups or green salads in place of croutons. You could even add a topping of crushed chips to casseroles before baking.

Hot Cranberry Punch

This rosy cranberry beverage is such a cozy comfort on cold autumn and winter days. It's a nice change of pace from the usual hot chocolate, too. Every glassful gets a tongue-tingling twist from tangy fruit juices and Red Hot candies.

—LAURA BURGESS BALLWIN, MO

PREP: 10 MIN. • **COOK:** 2 HOURS
MAKES: 3½ QUARTS

- 8 cups hot water
- 1½ cups sugar
- 4 cups cranberry juice
- ¾ cup orange juice
- ¼ cup lemon juice
- 12 whole cloves, optional
- ½ cup Red Hot candies

In a 5-qt. slow cooker, combine water, sugar and juices; stir until sugar is dissolved. If desired, place cloves in a double thickness of cheesecloth; bring up corners of cloth and tie with string to form a bag. Add spice bag and Red Hots to slow cooker. Cover and cook on low for 2-3 hours or until heated through. Before serving, discard spice bag and stir punch.

DID YOU KNOW?

A festive garnish is an easy way to give beverages extra pizzazz. Cinnamon sticks and orange slices make great accents for glasses of Hot Cranberry Punch. You could also perch a mini skewer of cranberries across the top of each glass, or cut out fun shapes from orange or lemon rinds using mini cookie cutters.

Chai Tea

An enticing sweet-spicy aroma wafts from the kitchen as this pleasantly flavored chai cooks. Then I take a sip—sheer bliss!
—**CRYSTAL BRUNS** ILIFF, CO

PREP: 20 MIN. • **COOK:** 8 HOURS
MAKES: 12 SERVINGS (3 QUARTS)

3½ ounces fresh gingerroot, peeled and thinly sliced
25 whole cloves
15 cardamom pods, crushed
3 cinnamon sticks (3 inches)
3 whole peppercorns
3½ quarts water
8 individual black tea bags
1 can (14 ounces) sweetened condensed milk

1. Place the ginger, cloves, cardamom, cinnamon sticks and peppercorns on a double thickness of cheesecloth; bring up the corners of cloth and tie with string to form a bag. Add the spice bag and water to a 5- or 6-qt. slow cooker. Cover and cook on low for 8 hours.

2. Add tea bags; cover and steep for 3-5 minutes. Discard tea bags and spice bag. Stir in sweetened condensed milk; heat through. Serve warm.

DID YOU KNOW?

Fresh gingerroot is sold in the produce department of grocery stores. This root should have a smooth, wrinkle-free skin and a spicy fragrance. Wrapped in a paper towel and placed in a plastic bag, unpeeled gingerroot may be refrigerated for up to 3 weeks. It may also be tightly wrapped and frozen for up to 2 months.

**Easy Slow Cooker
Mac & Cheese, p. 37**

CHAPTER 2

SIDE DISHES

These amazing accompaniments just might steal the spotlight.

Loaded Mashed Potatoes

Each year, my mother made her dressed-up mashed potatoes as part of our Thanksgiving dinner. When I started cooking for my own family, I carried on her tradition. I really love the convenience of using my slow cooker to prepare this special dish, and everyone at the table requests a big scoop.

—**ANN NOLTE** RIVERVIEW, FL

PREP: 25 MIN. + CHILLING
COOK: 3 HOURS • **MAKES:** 10 SERVINGS

- 3 pounds potatoes (about 9 medium), peeled and cubed
- 1 package (8 ounces) cream cheese, softened
- 1 cup (8 ounces) sour cream
- 1/2 cup butter, cubed
- 1/4 cup 2% milk
- 1 1/2 cups (6 ounces) shredded cheddar cheese
- 1 1/2 cups (6 ounces) shredded pepper jack cheese
- 1/2 pound bacon strips, cooked and crumbled
- 4 green onions, chopped
- 1/2 teaspoon onion powder
- 1/2 teaspoon garlic powder

1. Place the potatoes in a Dutch oven and cover with water. Bring to a boil. Reduce heat; cover and cook for 10-15 minutes or until tender. Drain.

2. Mash potatoes with the cream cheese, sour cream, butter and milk. Stir in the cheeses, bacon, onions and seasonings. Transfer to a large bowl; cover and refrigerate overnight.

3. Transfer the mixture to a greased 3- or 4-qt. slow cooker. Cover and cook on low for 3 to 3 1/2 hours.

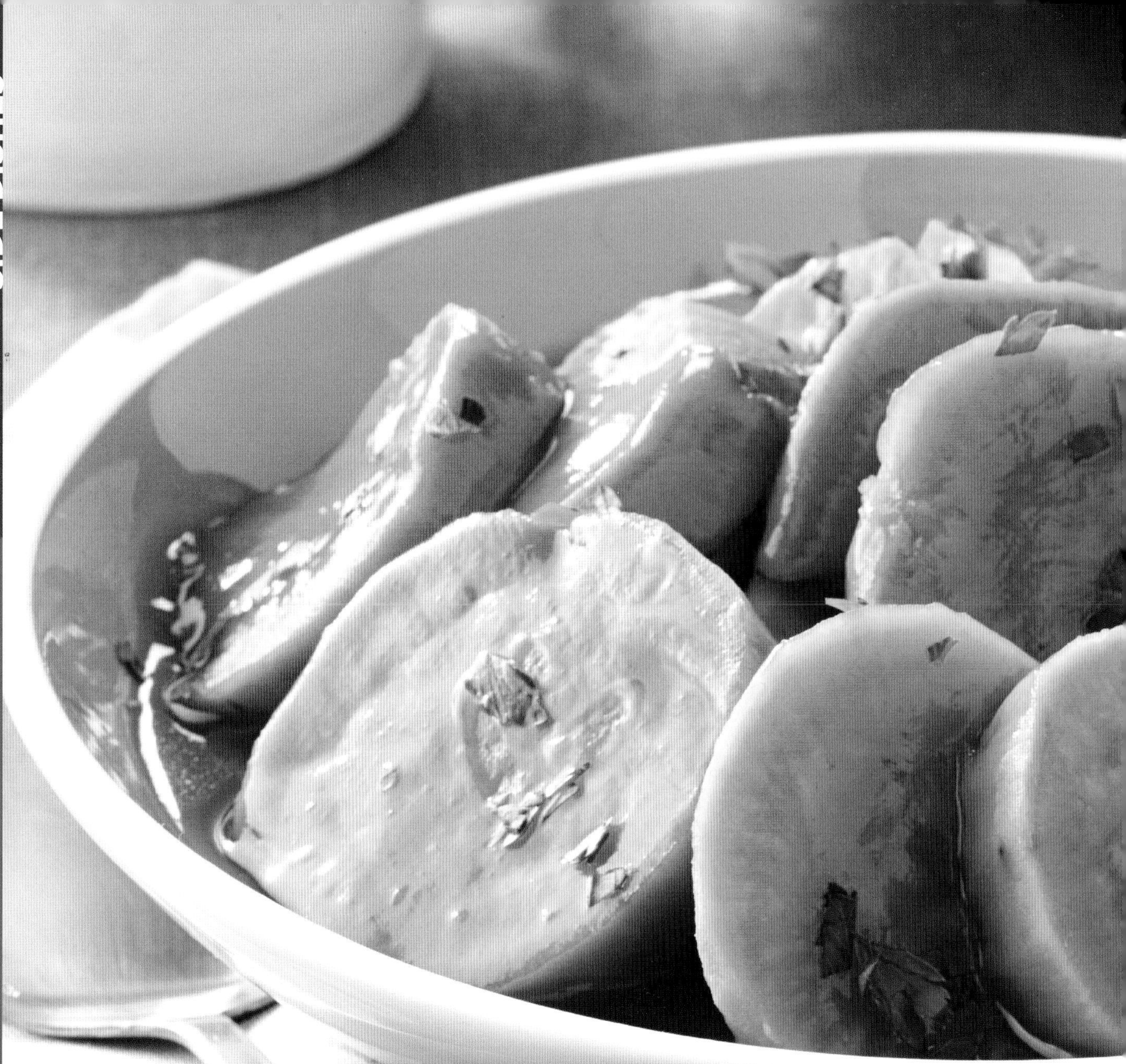

Slow Cooker Candied Sweet Potatoes

A classic Southern favorite, candied sweet potatoes are always popular at potlucks and other gatherings. I adjusted my recipe so it can be made in a slow cooker. For a pretty pop of contrasting color, sprinkle on some minced fresh parsley before serving.

—DEIRDRE COX KANSAS CITY, MO

PREP: 20 MIN. • **COOK:** 5 HOURS
MAKES: 12 SERVINGS (¾ CUP EACH)

- 1 cup packed brown sugar
- 1 cup sugar
- 8 medium sweet potatoes, peeled and cut into ½-inch slices
- ¼ cup butter, melted
- 2 teaspoons vanilla extract
- ¼ teaspoon salt
- 2 tablespoons cornstarch
- 2 tablespoons cold water
  Minced fresh parsley, optional

1. In a small bowl, combine the sugars. In a greased 5-qt. slow cooker, layer a third of the sweet potatoes; sprinkle with a third of the sugar mixture. Repeat the layers twice.

2. In a small bowl, combine butter, vanilla and salt; drizzle over the sweet potatoes. Cover and cook on low for 5-6 hours or until sweet potatoes are tender.

3. Using a slotted spoon, transfer the sweet potatoes to a serving dish; keep warm. Pour the cooking juices into a small saucepan; bring to a boil. In a small bowl, combine the cornstarch and cold water until smooth; stir into pan. Return to a boil, stirring constantly; cook and stir for 1-2 minutes or until thickened. Spoon over sweet potatoes.

4. Sprinkle sweet potatoes with parsley if desired.

Cheesy Spinach

My daughter often brings this cheese-and-spinach medley to church suppers. Even people who usually shy away from green veggies like this flavorful dish once they taste it.

—FRANCES MOORE DECATUR, IL

PREP: 10 MIN. • **COOK:** 5 HOURS
MAKES: 6-8 SERVINGS

- 2 packages (10 ounces each) frozen chopped spinach, thawed and well drained
- 2 cups (16 ounces) 4% cottage cheese
- 1½ cups cubed process cheese (Velveeta)
- 3 eggs, lightly beaten
- ¼ cup butter, cubed
- ¼ cup all-purpose flour
- 1 teaspoon salt

In a large bowl, combine all ingredients. Pour into a greased 3-qt. slow cooker. Cover and cook on high for 1 hour. Reduce heat to low; cook 4-5 hours longer or until a knife inserted near the center comes out clean.

DID YOU KNOW?

Brown and white eggs have the same nutritional value and cook the same. The color of the egg is based on the breed of the chicken. It's best to store all eggs in their carton on an inside refrigerator shelf, not in a compartment on the door. The carton cushions the eggs and helps prevent moisture loss and odor absorption.

Easy Slow Cooker Mac & Cheese

My sons always cheer, "You're the best mom in the world!" when I surprise them with bowls of ooey-gooey macaroni and cheese. It doesn't get much better than that!

—**HEIDI FLEEK** HAMBURG, PA

PREP: 25 MIN. • **COOK:** 1 HOUR
MAKES: 8 SERVINGS

- 2 cups uncooked elbow macaroni
- 1 can (10¾ ounces) condensed cheddar cheese soup, undiluted
- 1 cup 2% milk
- ½ cup sour cream
- ¼ cup butter, cubed
- ½ teaspoon onion powder
- ¼ teaspoon white pepper
- ⅛ teaspoon salt
- 1 cup (4 ounces) shredded cheddar cheese
- 1 cup (4 ounces) shredded fontina cheese
- 1 cup (4 ounces) shredded provolone cheese

1. Cook the macaroni according to the package directions for al dente. Meanwhile, in a large saucepan, combine the soup, milk, sour cream, butter and seasonings; cook and stir over medium-low heat until blended. Stir in cheeses until melted.

2. Drain macaroni; transfer to a greased 3-qt. slow cooker. Stir in cheese mixture. Cook, covered, on low 1-2 hours or until heated through.

Slow Cooker Mushroom Rice Pilaf

Flavored with portobello mushrooms, beef base, green onions and garlic, this tasty rice pilaf makes a wonderful side for many types of main dishes. Our family has enjoyed it countless times at barbecues and other get-togethers.

—AMY WILLIAMS RIALTO, CA

PREP: 20 MIN. • **COOK:** 3 HOURS
MAKES: 6 SERVINGS

- 1 cup medium grain rice
- 1/4 cup butter
- 6 green onions, chopped
- 2 garlic cloves, minced
- 1/2 pound sliced baby portobello mushrooms
- 2 cups warm water
- 4 teaspoons beef base

1. In a large skillet, saute the rice in the butter until lightly browned. Add green onions and garlic; cook and stir until tender. Stir in mushrooms.

2. Transfer to a 1½-qt. slow cooker. In a small bowl, whisk the water and beef base; pour over rice mixture. Cover and cook on low for 3 to 3½ hours or until the rice is tender and the liquid is absorbed. Fluff with a fork.

NOTE Look for beef base near the broth and bouillon.

Sweet & Spicy Beans

How much do my husband and I love these zesty beans? We eat them not only as a side dish, but also as a chunky dip with corn chips. This easy recipe requires only 10 minutes of prep work, so we can dig in just about any time the mood strikes.

—**SONDRA POPE** MOORESVILLE, NC

PREP: 10 MIN. • **COOK:** 5 HOURS
MAKES: 12 SERVINGS (⅔ CUP EACH)

1 can (16 ounces) kidney beans, rinsed and drained
1 can (15¼ ounces) whole kernel corn, drained
1 can (15 ounces) garbanzo beans or chickpeas, rinsed and drained
1 can (15 ounces) black beans, rinsed and drained
1 can (15 ounces) chili with beans
1 cup barbecue sauce
1 cup salsa
⅓ cup packed brown sugar
¼ teaspoon hot pepper sauce
Chopped green onions, optional

In a 4- or 5-qt. slow cooker, combine the first nine ingredients. Cover; cook on low for 5-6 hours. Top with green onions if desired.

TOP TIP

To soften brown sugar, place a slice of bread or an apple wedge with the sugar in a covered container for a few days. If you're in a hurry, microwave the sugar on high for 20-30 seconds. Repeat if necessary, but watch carefully because the sugar will begin to melt. Always store brown sugar in an airtight container.

Scalloped Taters

Here's a creamy, comforting side dish that tastes great with just about any main course. Thanks to convenience products such as frozen cubed hash browns, canned soup and packaged shredded cheese, assembly is a snap, too.

—LUCINDA WOLKER SOMERSET, PA

PREP: 10 MIN. • **COOK:** 3 HOURS
MAKES: 12 SERVINGS

1	package (2 pounds) frozen cubed hash brown potatoes
1	can (10¾ ounces) condensed cream of chicken soup, undiluted
1½	cups whole milk
1	cup (4 ounces) shredded cheddar cheese
½	cup plus 1 tablespoon butter, melted, divided
¼	cup dried minced onion
½	teaspoon salt
⅛	teaspoon pepper
¾	cup crushed cornflakes

1. In a large bowl, combine the cubed hash browns, soup, milk, cheese, ½ cup butter, onion, salt and pepper. Pour into a greased 5-qt. slow cooker. Cover and cook on low for 3-4 hours or until potatoes are tender.

2. Just before serving, combine the cornflake crumbs and remaining butter in a pie plate. Bake at 350° for 4-6 minutes or until golden brown. Stir the potatoes; sprinkle with crumb topping.

Spiced Acorn Squash

When I was working full-time, my hectic schedule didn't always allow me to cook the foods my family loved most. So I adapted many of our favorites for the slow cooker. This sweet-spicy treatment for acorn squash is one of them.
—**CAROL GRECO** CENTEREACH, NY

PREP: 15 MIN. • **COOK:** 3½ HOURS
MAKES: 4 SERVINGS

- ¾ cup packed brown sugar
- 1 teaspoon ground cinnamon
- 1 teaspoon ground nutmeg
- 2 small acorn squash, halved and seeded
- ¾ cup raisins
- 4 tablespoons butter
- ½ cup water

1. In a small bowl, mix the brown sugar, cinnamon and nutmeg; spoon into acorn squash halves. Sprinkle with raisins. Top each with 1 tablespoon butter. Wrap each half individually in heavy-duty foil, sealing tightly.

2. Pour the water into a 5-qt. slow cooker. Place squash in the slow cooker, cut side up (packets may be stacked). Cook, covered, on high 3½ to 4 hours or until squash is tender. Open foil carefully to allow steam to escape.

Black-Eyed Peas & Ham

We have these slow-cooked black-eyed peas regularly at our house. The cayenne and jalapeno pepper add a little zip.

—**DAWN FRIHAUF** FORT MORGAN, CO

PREP: 20 MIN. • **COOK:** 6 HOURS
MAKES: 12 SERVINGS (¾ CUP EACH)

- 1 package (16 ounces) dried black-eyed peas, rinsed and sorted
- ½ pound fully cooked boneless ham, finely chopped
- 1 medium onion, finely chopped
- 1 medium sweet red pepper, finely chopped
- 5 bacon strips, cooked and crumbled
- 1 large jalapeno pepper, seeded and finely chopped
- 2 garlic cloves, minced
- 1½ teaspoons ground cumin
- 1 teaspoon reduced-sodium chicken bouillon granules
- ½ teaspoon salt
- ½ teaspoon cayenne pepper
- ¼ teaspoon pepper
- 6 cups water
  Minced fresh cilantro, optional
  Hot cooked rice

In a 6-qt. slow cooker, combine the first 13 ingredients. Cover and cook on low for 6-8 hours or until the peas are tender. Sprinkle with cilantro if desired. Serve with rice.

NOTE Wear disposable gloves when cutting hot peppers; the oils can burn skin. Avoid touching your face.

Creamed Corn

Turn a few bags of plain frozen corn into a home-style delight. It's as simple as combining them with cream cheese, butter, sugar and salt, then turning on the slow cooker. I keep the recipe handy whenever I'm having a barbecue.

—**BARBARA BRIZENDINE** HARRISONVILLE, MO

PREP: 10 MIN. • **COOK:** 3 HOURS
MAKES: 5 SERVINGS

- 2 packages (one 16 ounces, one 10 ounces) frozen corn
- 1 package (8 ounces) cream cheese, softened and cubed
- 1/4 cup butter, cubed
- 1 tablespoon sugar
- 1/2 teaspoon salt

In a 3-qt. slow cooker coated with cooking spray, combine all ingredients. Cover and cook on low for 3 to 3½ hours or until the cheese is melted and the corn is tender. Stir just before serving.

TOP TIP

Unless your recipe instructs you to stir or add ingredients, do not lift the lid while your food is cooking in the slow cooker. The loss of steam that results can mean an extra 20-30 minutes of cooking time each time you lift the lid. Also, make sure the lid is well-placed and not tilted or askew; the steam during cooking creates a seal.

POTLUCK

Bacon & Sausage Stuffing

Inspired by my mother's wonderful recipe, this hearty stuffing smells heavenly while you're making it—and tastes even better.

—**SCOTT RUGH** PORTLAND, OR

PREP: 25 MIN.
COOK: 4 HOURS + STANDING
MAKES: 20 SERVINGS (¾ CUP EACH)

1	pound bulk pork sausage
1	pound thick-sliced bacon strips, chopped
½	cup butter, cubed
1	large onion, chopped
3	celery ribs, sliced
10½	cups unseasoned stuffing cubes
1	cup sliced fresh mushrooms
1	cup chopped fresh parsley
4	teaspoons dried sage leaves
4	teaspoons dried thyme
6	eggs
2	cans (10¾ ounces each) condensed cream of chicken soup, undiluted
1¼	cups chicken stock

1. In a large skillet, cook sausage over medium heat for 6-8 minutes or until no longer pink, breaking into crumbles. Remove with a slotted spoon; drain on paper towels. Discard sausage drippings.

2. Add bacon to pan; cook over medium heat until crisp. Remove to paper towels to drain. Discard bacon drippings. Wipe out pan. In same pan, heat the butter over medium-high heat. Add onion and celery; cook and stir 6-8 minutes or until tender. Remove from heat.

3. In a large bowl, combine unseasoned stuffing cubes, sausage, bacon, onion mixture, mushrooms, parsley, sage and thyme. In a small bowl, whisk the eggs, cream of chicken soup and chicken stock; pour over the stuffing mixture and toss to coat.

4. Transfer to a greased 6-qt. slow cooker. Cook, covered, on low 4-5 hours or until a thermometer reads 160°. Remove lid; let stand 15 minutes before serving.

Slow Cooker Turkey Chili, p. 54

CHAPTER 3

SOUPS, STEWS & CHILI

Come home to a bowlful of ready-to-eat comfort food.

Slow Cooker Turkey Chili

I love this chili because I can prepare it before I leave in the morning, then enjoy a hearty dinner when I get home in the evening. I can make a big batch to freeze, too!

—**TERRI CRANDALL** GARDNERVILLE, NV

PREP: 30 MIN. • **COOK:** 7¼ HOURS
MAKES: 8 SERVINGS (2¾ QUARTS)

- 2 tablespoons olive oil
- 1½ pounds ground turkey
- 1 medium onion, chopped
- 2 tablespoons ground ancho chili pepper
- 1 tablespoon chili powder
- 1½ teaspoons salt
- 1½ teaspoons ground cumin
- 1½ teaspoons paprika
- 2 cans (14½ ounces each) fire-roasted diced tomatoes, undrained
- 1 medium sweet yellow pepper, chopped
- 1 medium sweet red pepper, chopped
- 1 can (4 ounces) chopped green chilies
- 1 garlic clove, minced
- 1 cup brewed coffee
- ¾ cup dry red wine or chicken broth
- 1 can (16 ounces) kidney beans, rinsed and drained
- 1 can (15 ounces) white kidney or cannellini beans, rinsed and drained
  Sliced avocado and chopped green onions

1. In a large skillet, heat oil over medium heat. Add ground turkey and onion; cook 8-10 minutes or until meat is no longer pink, breaking up meat into crumbles.

2. Transfer to a 5-qt. slow cooker; stir in seasonings. Add fire-roasted tomatoes, sweet peppers, chilies and garlic; stir in coffee and wine.

3. Cook, covered, on low 7-9 hours. Stir in the beans; cook 15-20 minutes longer or until heated through. Top servings with avocado and green onions.

FREEZE OPTION Freeze the cooled chili in freezer containers. To use, partially thaw chili in refrigerator overnight. Heat through in a saucepan, stirring occasionally and adding broth or water if necessary.

Tempting Teriyaki Chicken Stew

When I tried coming up with a dinner dish that blends two of my favorite tastes—salty and sweet—this Asian-style chicken stew was the result. Add fresh-baked bread, biscuits or rolls on the side for a complete meal.

—AMY SIEGEL CLIFTON, NJ

PREP: 20 MIN. • **COOK:** 7 HOURS
MAKES: 6 SERVINGS

1 tablespoon olive oil
6 bone-in chicken thighs (about 2 pounds)
2 medium sweet potatoes, cut into 1-inch pieces
3 medium carrots, cut into 1-inch pieces
1 medium parsnip, peeled and cut into 1-inch pieces
1 medium onion, sliced
1 cup apricot preserves
½ cup maple syrup
½ cup teriyaki sauce
½ teaspoon ground ginger
⅛ teaspoon cayenne pepper
2 tablespoons cornstarch
2 tablespoons cold water

1. In a large skillet, heat the olive oil over medium-high heat; brown the chicken on both sides. Place the vegetables in a 4-qt. slow cooker; add chicken. In a small bowl, mix the apricot preserves, maple syrup, teriyaki sauce, ginger and cayenne; pour over chicken.

2. Cover and cook on low for 6-8 hours or until chicken is tender. Remove chicken and vegetables to a platter; keep warm.

3. Transfer the cooking liquid to a small saucepan. Skim fat. Bring the cooking liquid to a boil. In a small bowl, combine cornstarch and cold water until smooth; gradually stir into the pan. Return to a boil, stirring constantly; cook and stir for 2 minutes or until thickened. Serve with chicken and vegetables.

Slow Cooker Beef Vegetable Stew

I tweaked my mom's wonderful beef stew recipe so I could make it in the slow cooker. When I come home after a busy day, all I have to do is mix in the last few ingredients before sitting down to a big bowl of comfort food. Sometimes I sprinkle on a little Parmesan cheese as the finishing touch.

—MARCELLA WEST WASHBURN, IL

PREP: 20 MIN. • **COOK:** 6½ HOURS
MAKES: 8 SERVINGS (3 QUARTS)

1½ pounds boneless beef chuck roast, cut into 1-inch cubes
3 medium potatoes, peeled and cubed
3 cups hot water
1½ cups fresh baby carrots
1 can (10¾ ounces) condensed tomato soup, undiluted
1 medium onion, chopped
1 celery rib, chopped
2 tablespoons Worcestershire sauce
1 tablespoon browning sauce, optional
2 teaspoons beef bouillon granules
1 garlic clove, minced
1 teaspoon sugar
¾ teaspoon salt
¼ teaspoon pepper
¼ cup cornstarch
¾ cup cold water
2 cups frozen peas, thawed

1. Place the beef, potatoes, hot water, carrots, tomato soup, onion, celery, Worcestershire sauce, browning sauce if desired, beef bouillon granules, garlic, sugar, salt and pepper in a 5- or 6-qt. slow cooker. Cover; cook on low for 6-8 hours or until meat is tender.

2. Combine the cornstarch and cold water in a small bowl until smooth; gradually stir into the stew. Stir in the peas. Cover and cook on high for 30 minutes or until thickened.

Bean & Beef Slow-Cooked Chili

My hearty chili is full of chunky ingredients, but we build it up even more with toppings like pico de gallo, red onion and cilantro.
—**MALLORY LYNCH** MADISON, WI

PREP: 20 MIN. • **COOK:** 6 HOURS
MAKES: 6 SERVINGS (2¼ QUARTS)

- 1 pound lean ground beef (90% lean)
- 1 large sweet onion, chopped
- 3 garlic cloves, minced
- 2 cans (14½ ounces each) diced tomatoes with mild green chilies
- 2 cans (15 ounces each) pinto beans, rinsed and drained
- 2 cans (15 ounces each) black beans, rinsed and drained
- 2 to 3 tablespoons chili powder
- 2 teaspoons ground cumin
- ½ teaspoon salt
  Optional toppings: sour cream, chopped red onion and minced fresh cilantro

1. In a large skillet, cook beef, onion and garlic over medium heat 6-8 minutes or until beef is no longer pink, breaking up beef into crumbles; drain.

2. Transfer the beef mixture to a 5-qt. slow cooker. Drain one can tomatoes, discarding liquid; add to slow cooker. Stir in beans, chili powder, cumin, salt and remaining tomatoes. Cook, covered, on low 6-8 hours to allow flavors to blend.

3. Mash beans to desired consistency. Serve with toppings as desired.

FREEZE OPTION Freeze the cooled chili in freezer containers. To use, partially thaw in refrigerator overnight. Heat through in a saucepan, stirring occasionally and adding a little water if necessary.

TOP TIP

Have leftover chili but not enough to serve by the bowlful as a second meal? Spoon the extra chili over baked potatoes, or use it to make chili dogs. You could even stir process cheese (Velveeta) into the chili to make a hot dip you can eat with tortilla chips.

Loaded Baked Potato Soup

The only thing that beats the taste of this comforting potato soup is the fact that it simmers on its own all day.

—BARBARA BLEIGH COLONIAL HEIGHTS, VA

PREP: 35 MIN. • **COOK:** 6 HOURS
MAKES: 10 SERVINGS

    2   large onions, chopped
    3   tablespoons butter
    2   tablespoons all-purpose flour
    2   cups water, divided
    4   cups chicken broth
    2   medium potatoes, peeled and diced
 1½   cups mashed potato flakes
  ½   pound sliced bacon, cooked and crumbled
  ¾   teaspoon pepper
  ½   teaspoon salt
  ½   teaspoon dried basil
  ⅛   teaspoon dried thyme
    1   cup half-and-half cream
  ½   cup shredded cheddar cheese
    2   green onions, sliced

1. In a large skillet, saute the onions in butter until tender. Stir in flour. Gradually stir in 1 cup water. Bring to a boil; cook and stir for 2 minutes or until thickened. Transfer to a 5-qt. slow cooker.

2. Add the chicken broth, potatoes, potato flakes, bacon, pepper, salt, basil, thyme and remaining water. Cover and cook on low for 6-8 hours or until the potatoes are tender. Stir in half-and-half cream; heat through. Garnish with cheese and green onions.

SOUPS, STEWS & CHILI 63

Shrimp Chowder

Take just 15 minutes to get this rich, creamy seafood chowder going in the afternoon. You'll be glad you did! A brimming bowlful is so good for dinner, especially on a chilly day.

—WILL ZUNIO GRETNA, LA

PREP: 15 MIN. • **COOK:** 3½ HOURS
MAKES: 12 SERVINGS (3 QUARTS)

½ cup chopped onion
2 teaspoons butter
2 cans (12 ounces each) evaporated milk
2 cans (10¾ ounces each) condensed cream of potato soup, undiluted
2 cans (10¾ ounces each) condensed cream of chicken soup, undiluted
1 can (7 ounces) white or shoepeg corn, drained
1 teaspoon Creole seasoning
½ teaspoon garlic powder
2 pounds peeled and deveined cooked small shrimp
1 package (3 ounces) cream cheese, cubed

1. In a small skillet, saute onion in butter until tender. In a 5-qt. slow cooker, combine the onion, milk, soups, corn, Creole seasoning and garlic powder.

2. Cover and cook on low for 3 hours. Stir in shrimp and cream cheese. Cook 30 minutes longer or until shrimp are heated through and cheese is melted. Stir to blend.

NOTE The following spices may be substituted for 1 teaspoon Creole seasoning: ¼ teaspoon each salt, garlic powder and paprika; and a pinch each of dried thyme, ground cumin and cayenne pepper.

Slow-Cooked Fish Stew

Tender chunks of cod, colorful vegetables and plenty of seasonings make a stew that looks and tastes special. To add a little extra richness and flavor, garnish each serving with grated cheddar cheese.
—**JANE WHITTAKER** PENSACOLA, FL

PREP: 25 MIN. • **COOK:** 6½ HOURS
MAKES: 8 SERVINGS (3 QUARTS)

1 pound potatoes (about 2 medium), peeled and finely chopped
1 package (10 ounces) frozen corn, thawed
1½ cups frozen lima beans, thawed
1 large onion, finely chopped
1 celery rib, finely chopped
1 medium carrot, finely chopped
4 garlic cloves, minced
1 bay leaf
1 teaspoon lemon-pepper seasoning
1 teaspoon dried parsley flakes
1 teaspoon dried rosemary, crushed
½ teaspoon salt
1½ cups vegetable or chicken broth
1 can (10¾ ounces) condensed cream of celery soup, undiluted
½ cup white wine or additional vegetable broth
1 pound cod fillets, cut into 1-inch pieces
1 can (14½ ounces) diced tomatoes, undrained
1 can (12 ounces) fat-free evaporated milk

1. In a 5-qt. slow cooker, combine the first 15 ingredients. Cook, covered, on low 6-8 hours or until potatoes are tender.

2. Remove bay leaf. Stir in cod, tomatoes and milk; cook, covered, 30-35 minutes longer or until fish just begins to flake easily with a fork.

TOP TIP

Buy fresh fish fillets that have firm, elastic and moist-looking flesh and a mild smell. Avoid fish with a strong fishy odor, bruised skin and flesh with drying edges. Buy frozen fish in packages that are solidly frozen, tightly sealed and free of freezer burn and odor. Thaw frozen fish in its original package in the refrigerator.

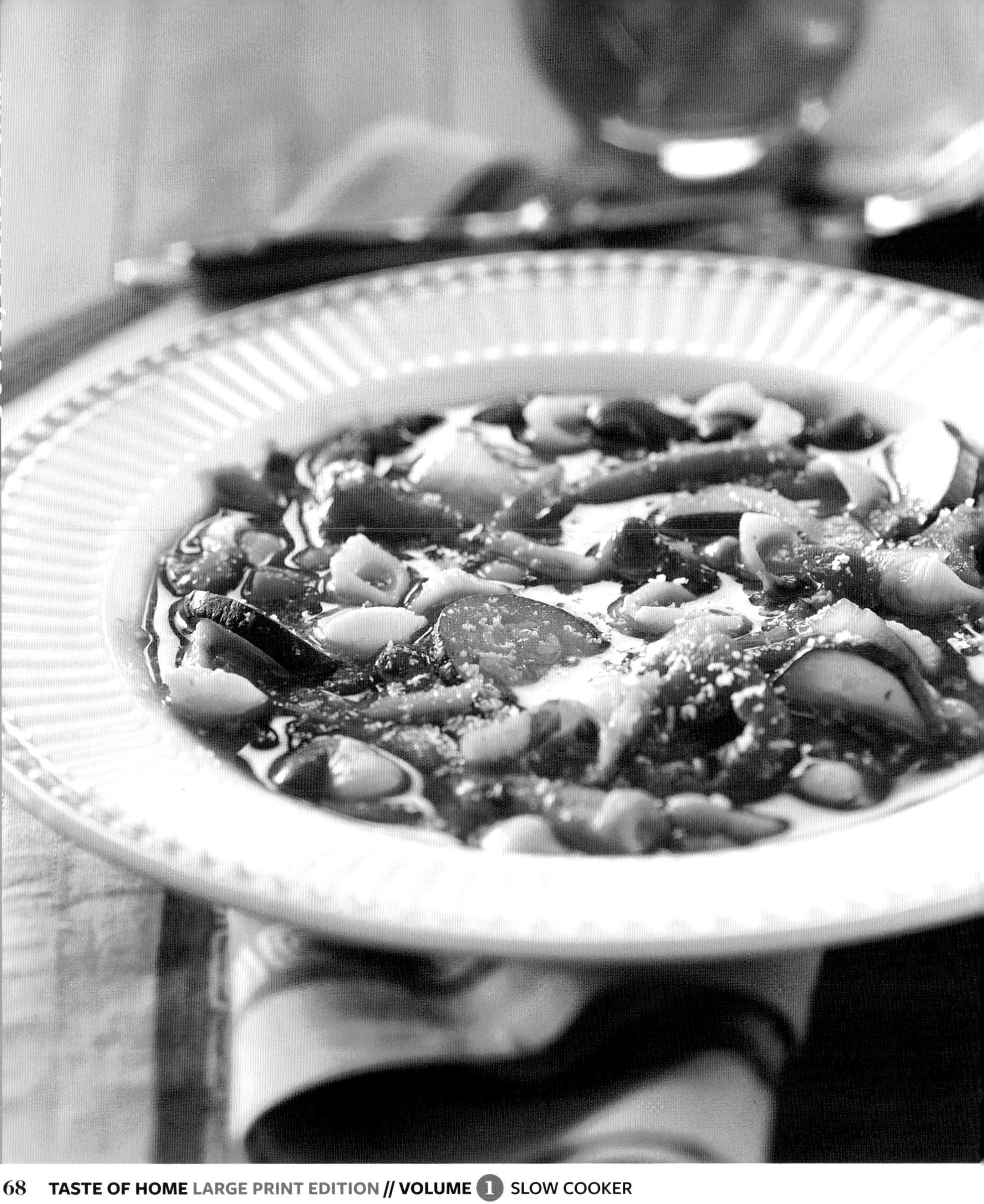

Vegetable Minestrone

My husband and I enjoy the minestrone at our favorite Italian restaurant so much, we experimented until we replicated that soup at home. Now we can indulge anytime! To make the recipe vegetarian, replace the beef broth with vegetable broth.

—ALICE PEACOCK GRANDVIEW, MO

PREP: 15 MIN. • **COOK:** 6½ HOURS
MAKES: 8 SERVINGS (2½ QUARTS)

- 2 cans (14½ ounces each) beef broth
- 1 can (16 ounces) kidney beans, rinsed and drained
- 1 can (15 ounces) great northern beans, rinsed and drained
- 1 can (14½ ounces) Italian-style stewed tomatoes
- 1 large onion, chopped
- 1 medium zucchini, thinly sliced
- 1 medium carrot, shredded
- ¾ cup tomato juice
- 1 teaspoon dried basil
- ¾ teaspoon dried oregano
- ¼ teaspoon garlic powder
- 1 cup frozen cut green beans, thawed
- ½ cup frozen chopped spinach, thawed
- ½ cup small shell pasta
- ½ cup shredded Parmesan cheese

1. In a 4- or 5-qt. slow cooker, combine the first 11 ingredients. Cover and cook on low for 6-7 hours or until vegetables are tender.

2. Stir in the green beans, spinach and shell pasta. Cover; cook for 30 minutes or until heated through. Sprinkle with Parmesan cheese.

TOP TIP

Some recipes recommend that you cook pasta according to the package directions and then stir it into the slow cooker just before serving. In general, small types of pasta such as orzo and small shells may be cooked in the slow cooker. To keep them from becoming mushy, add them during the last hour of cooking.

Lemon Chicken & Rice Soup

Give your taste buds a tongue-tingling change of pace from the usual chicken and rice soup. This citrus version mixes in lemon slices, juice and grated peel for a tangy twist.
—**KRISTIN CHERRY** BOTHELL, WA

PREP: 35 MIN. • **COOK:** 4¼ HOURS
MAKES: 12 SERVINGS (4 QUARTS)

- 2 tablespoons olive oil
- 2 pounds boneless skinless chicken breasts, cut into ½-inch pieces
- 5 cans (14½ ounces each) reduced-sodium chicken broth
- 8 cups coarsely chopped Swiss chard, kale or spinach
- 2 large carrots, finely chopped
- 1 small onion, chopped
- 1 medium lemon, halved and thinly sliced
- ¼ cup lemon juice
- 4 teaspoons grated lemon peel
- ½ teaspoon pepper
- 4 cups cooked brown rice

1. In a large skillet, heat 1 tablespoon oil over medium-high heat. Add half of the chicken; cook and stir until browned. Transfer to a 6-qt. slow cooker. Repeat with remaining oil and chicken.

2. Stir broth, vegetables, lemon slices, lemon juice, peel and pepper into chicken. Cook, covered, on low 4-5 hours or until chicken is tender. Stir in rice; heat through.

Momma's Turkey Stew with Dumplings

My mother always used our Thanksgiving leftovers to prepare a simple turkey stew full of wholesome ingredients. To this day, it's one of my favorite meals.

—STEPHANIE RABBITT-SCHAPP

CINCINNATI, OH

PREP: 20 MIN. • **COOK:** 6½ HOURS
MAKES: 6 SERVINGS

- 3 cups shredded cooked turkey
- 1 large sweet onion, chopped
- 1 large potato, peeled and cubed
- 2 large carrots, chopped
- 2 celery ribs, chopped
- 2 bay leaves
- 1 teaspoon salt
- ½ teaspoon poultry seasoning
- ½ teaspoon dried thyme
- ¼ teaspoon pepper
- 1 carton (32 ounces) chicken broth
- ⅓ cup cold water
- 3 tablespoons cornstarch
- ½ cup frozen corn, thawed
- ½ cup frozen peas, thawed
- 1 cup biscuit/baking mix
- ⅓ cup 2% milk

1. In a 6-qt. slow cooker, combine the first 10 ingredients; stir in the chicken broth. Cover and cook on low for 6-7 hours.

2. Remove the bay leaves. In a small bowl, mix water and cornstarch until smooth; stir into the turkey mixture. Add the corn and peas. Cover and cook on high until mixture reaches a simmer.

3. Meanwhile, in a small bowl, mix the baking mix and milk just until moistened. Drop by rounded tablespoonfuls on top of simmering liquid. Reduce heat to low; cover and cook for 20-25 minutes or until a toothpick inserted in a dumpling comes out clean.

HOW TO

MAKE YOUR OWN SEASONING

Want to prepare a recipe that calls for poultry seasoning but don't have any in your pantry? Skip the extra trip to the store and make your own at home with this easy-as-can-be recipe that yields 1 teaspoon of poultry seasoning: Simply combine ¾ teaspoon rubbed sage and ¼ teaspoon dried thyme or marjoram.

Slow-Cooked Split Pea Soup

I've been making this classic for so many years, I've become known for it. When I'm at a dinner featuring ham, the hostess often sends me home with the ham bone and a bag of peas so I can cook a batch of my soup.
—**SUSAN SIMONS** EATONVILLE, WA

PREP: 15 MIN. • **COOK:** 7 HOURS
MAKES: 8 SERVINGS (ABOUT 3 QUARTS)

1   meaty ham bone or 2 pounds
    smoked ham hocks
1   package (16 ounces) dried green
    split peas
1   pound potatoes, peeled and cubed
    (about 3 cups)
1   large onion, chopped
2   medium carrots, chopped
1   tablespoon dried celery flakes
½   teaspoon garlic powder
½   teaspoon dried thyme
½   teaspoon dried basil
¼   teaspoon lemon-pepper seasoning
⅛   teaspoon dried marjoram
1   bay leaf
6   cups reduced-sodium chicken broth

1. In a 4- or 5-qt. slow cooker, combine all ingredients. Cook, covered, on low 7-9 hours or until peas are tender.

2. Remove the ham bone from the soup. When cool enough to handle, remove the meat from ham bone; discard the bone. Cut the meat into cubes and return to the soup or save the meat for another use. Remove bay leaf.

FREEZE OPTION Freeze the cooled soup in freezer containers. To use, partially thaw in refrigerator overnight. Heat through in a saucepan, stirring occasionally and adding a little broth if necessary.

Slow Cooker BBQ Ham Sandwiches, p. 82

CHAPTER 4

SANDWICHES

Pile 'em high with hearty ingredients from the slow cooker.

Easy Philly Cheesesteaks

We live in a rural area that doesn't have a lot of restaurants serving our favorite specialty foods. I thought it would be fun to come up with my own Philly cheesesteaks. Grab a bottle of steak sauce if you want an extra jolt of flavor.
—**LENETTE BENNETT** COMO, CO

PREP: 20 MIN. • **COOK:** 6 HOURS
MAKES: 6 SERVINGS

- 2 medium onions, halved and sliced
- 2 medium sweet red or green peppers, halved and sliced
- 1 beef top sirloin steak (1½ pounds), cut into thin strips
- 1 envelope onion soup mix
- 1 can (14½ ounces) reduced-sodium beef broth
- 6 hoagie buns, split
- 12 slices provolone cheese, halved
  Pickled hot cherry peppers, optional

1. Place the onions and red peppers in a 4- or 5-qt. slow cooker. Add the beef, soup mix and broth. Cook, covered, on low 6-8 hours or until meat is tender.

2. Arrange the hoagie buns on a baking sheet, cut side up. Using tongs, place the meat mixture on the bun bottoms; top with cheese.

3. Broil 2-3 in. from heat 30-60 seconds or until cheese is melted and bun tops are toasted. If desired, serve with cherry peppers.

Slow Cooker Meatball Sandwiches

My approach to making meatball sandwiches is a very simple one—cook Italian meatballs low and slow in marinara sauce, load them into hoagie buns and top them with provolone cheese and pepperoncinis. Delicious!

—STACIE NICHOLLS SPRING CREEK, NV

PREP: 5 MIN. • **COOK:** 3 HOURS
MAKES: 8 SERVINGS

- 2 packages (12 ounces each) frozen fully cooked Italian meatballs, thawed
- 2 jars (24 ounces each) marinara sauce
- 8 hoagie buns, split
- 8 slices provolone cheese
  Sliced pepperoncinis, optional

1. Place meatballs and sauce in a 3- or 4-qt. slow cooker. Cook, covered, on low 3-4 hours until the meatballs are heated through.

2. On each bun bottom, layer the meatballs, cheese and, if desired, pepperoncini; replace tops.

TOP TIP

These saucy slow-cooked meatball sandwiches get a little extra zip from pepperoncinis (pickled peppers). Look for them in the pickle and olive section of your grocery store.

Slow Cooker BBQ Ham Sandwiches

My friends love these barbecue ham sandwiches and often ask me to make them. The recipe is so popular, it's usually the first one I reach for when I need something for a potluck.

—**DANA KNOX** BUTLER, PA

PREP: 20 MIN. • **COOK:** 2 HOURS
MAKES: 16 SERVINGS

3	cups ketchup
¾	cup chopped onion
¾	cup chopped green pepper
¾	cup packed brown sugar
½	cup lemon juice
⅓	cup Worcestershire sauce
1	tablespoon prepared mustard
1¼	teaspoons ground allspice
1½	teaspoons liquid smoke, optional
3	pounds thinly sliced deli ham
16	kaiser or ciabatta rolls, split

1. In a large saucepan, combine the first eight ingredients; if desired, stir in liquid smoke. Bring to a boil. Reduce the heat; simmer, uncovered, 5 minutes, stirring occasionally.

2. Place the ham in a 5- or 6-qt. slow cooker. Add the sauce; stir gently to combine. Cook, covered, on low 2-3 hours or until heated through. Serve on rolls.

Hearty Italian Sandwiches

I've been making these Italian classics for years. They quickly draw a crowd because the sweet-spicy meat mixture of ground beef and sausage smells as good as it tastes.
—ELAINE KRUPSKY LAS VEGAS, NV

PREP: 20 MIN. • **COOK:** 6 HOURS
MAKES: 8 SERVINGS

$1\frac{1}{2}$ pounds lean ground beef (90% lean)
$1\frac{1}{2}$ pounds bulk Italian sausage
  2   large onions, sliced
  2   large green peppers, sliced
  2   large sweet red peppers, sliced
  1   teaspoon salt
  1   teaspoon pepper
 $\frac{1}{4}$ teaspoon crushed red pepper flakes
  8   sandwich rolls, split
     Shredded Monterey Jack cheese, optional

1. In a Dutch oven, cook the beef and Italian sausage over medium heat until no longer pink, breaking into crumbles; drain. Place a third of the onions and peppers in a 5-qt. slow cooker; top with half of the meat mixture. Repeat layers; top with remaining vegetables. Sprinkle with salt, pepper and pepper flakes.

2. Cover and cook on low for 6 hours or until the vegetables are tender. With a slotted spoon, serve about 1 cup of meat and vegetables on each roll. Top with cheese if desired. Use pan juices for dipping if desired.

Shredded Barbecue Beef Sandwiches

I serve my sandwiches with coleslaw as a cool counterpoint. It's good as a side dish or even right on the beef. If you have leftover meat, freeze it for an easy meal another day.
—**BUNNY PALMERTREE** CARROLLTON, MS

PREP: 10 MIN. • **COOK:** 10 HOURS
MAKES: 16 SERVINGS

---

1   can (10½ ounces) condensed beef broth, undiluted
1   cup ketchup
½   cup packed brown sugar
½   cup lemon juice
3   tablespoons steak sauce
2   garlic cloves, minced
1   teaspoon pepper
1   teaspoon Worcestershire sauce
1   beef eye round roast (3½ pounds), cut in half
1   teaspoon salt
16 sandwich buns, split
    Dill pickle slices, optional

1. In a small bowl, whisk the first eight ingredients. Pour half of mixture into a 5-qt. slow cooker. Sprinkle beef with salt; add to slow cooker and top with remaining broth mixture.

2. Cover and cook on low for 10-12 hours or until meat is tender. Shred meat with two forks and return to slow cooker. Using a slotted spoon, place ½ cup beef mixture on each bun. Top with pickles if desired.

Mini Teriyaki Turkey Sandwiches

Preparing the turkey for these snack-size sandwiches is a snap using my slow cooker.
—**AMANDA HOOP** SEAMAN, OH

PREP: 20 MIN. • **COOK:** 5½ HOURS
MAKES: 20 SERVINGS

2	boneless skinless turkey breast halves (2 pounds each)
⅔	cup packed brown sugar
⅔	cup reduced-sodium soy sauce
¼	cup cider vinegar
3	garlic cloves, minced
1	tablespoon minced fresh gingerroot
½	teaspoon pepper
2	tablespoons cornstarch
2	tablespoons cold water
20	Hawaiian sweet rolls
2	tablespoons butter, melted

1. Place turkey in a 5- or 6-qt. slow cooker. In a small bowl, combine brown sugar, soy sauce, cider vinegar, garlic, ginger and pepper; pour over turkey. Cook, covered, on low 5-6 hours or until meat is tender.

2. Remove the turkey from slow cooker. In a small bowl, mix cornstarch and cold water until smooth; gradually stir into cooking liquid. When cool enough to handle, shred the meat with two forks and return meat to slow cooker. Cook, covered, on high 30-35 minutes or until sauce is thickened.

3. Preheat oven to 325°. Split Hawaiian sweet rolls and brush the cut sides with butter; place on an ungreased baking sheet, cut side up. Bake 8-10 minutes or until toasted and golden brown. Spoon ⅓ cup turkey mixture on the bottoms of rolls. Replace the tops.

HOW TO

SHRED MEAT FOR SANDWICHES

Remove the cooked meat from the slow cooker or cooking pan, using a slotted spoon if needed. Reserve the cooking liquid if the recipe directs. Place the meat in a shallow pan. Holding a fork in each hand, pull the meat into thin shreds. Return the meat to the slow cooker or cooking pan to warm the meat or use it as directed.

Tropical Pulled Pork Sliders

I used what I had in my cupboard to make pulled pork sliders, and I was thrilled with the results. Tropical ingredients turned an inexpensive cut of meat into something special.

—SHELLY MITCHELL GRESHAM, OR

PREP: 15 MIN. • **COOK:** 8 HOURS
MAKES: 12 SERVINGS

1 boneless pork shoulder butt roast (3 pounds)
2 garlic cloves, minced
½ teaspoon lemon-pepper seasoning
1 can (20 ounces) unsweetened crushed pineapple, undrained
½ cup orange juice
1 jar (16 ounces) mango salsa
24 whole wheat dinner rolls, split

1. Rub roast with garlic and lemon pepper. Transfer to a 4-qt. slow cooker; top with pineapple and orange juice. Cook, covered, on low 8-10 hours or until meat is tender.

2. Remove the roast; cool slightly. Skim fat from cooking juices. Shred the pork with two forks. Return pork and cooking juices to slow cooker. Stir in salsa; heat through. Serve with rolls.

DID YOU KNOW?

Today's pork is easier than ever to cook because it is lean and tender. Due to animal feeding and breeding changes over the last 25 years, the fat content has been reduced.

Turkey Sloppy Joes

Chili sauce, garlic, jalapeno pepper and more bring mouthwatering flavor to sloppy joes made with ground turkey. Add refreshing avocado slices on top to balance the spice.

—**NICHOLE JONES** IDAHO FALLS, ID

PREP: 35 MIN. • **COOK:** 4 HOURS
MAKES: 8 SERVINGS

1½ pounds lean ground turkey
2 medium onions, finely chopped
4 garlic cloves, minced
1 jar (12 ounces) chili sauce
1 jalapeno pepper, seeded and chopped
1 tablespoon Worcestershire sauce
2 teaspoons dried oregano
1 teaspoon ground cumin
1 teaspoon paprika
½ teaspoon salt
½ teaspoon pepper
2 cups (8 ounces) shredded Monterey Jack cheese
8 onion rolls, split
2 medium ripe avocados, peeled and thinly sliced

1. In a large skillet coated with cooking spray, cook the turkey, onions and garlic over medium heat until meat is no longer pink; drain.

2. Transfer to a 1½-qt. slow cooker. Stir in the chili sauce, jalapeno pepper, Worcestershire sauce, oregano, cumin, paprika, salt and pepper. Cover; cook on low for 4-5 hours or until heated through. Just before serving, stir in cheese. Serve on rolls topped with avocado.

NOTE Wear disposable gloves when cutting hot peppers; the oils can burn skin. Avoid touching your face.

TOP TIP

The easiest avocados to peel and slice are those that are ripe yet firm. (Very ripe, soft avocados are best for mashing.) To quickly ripen an avocado, place it in a paper bag with an apple. Poke the bag with a toothpick in several spots and leave at room temperature. The avocado should be ripe in 1 to 3 days.

BBQ Chicken Sliders

Brining the chicken overnight makes it taste exceptionally good. If you're serving a side of coleslaw, add a scoop to your sandwich.
—**RACHEL KUNKEL** SCHELL CITY, MO

PREP: 25 MIN. + BRINING • **COOK:** 4 HOURS
MAKES: 8 SERVINGS (2 SLIDERS EACH)

BRINE
1½ quarts water
¼ cup packed brown sugar
2 tablespoons salt
1 tablespoon liquid smoke
2 garlic cloves, minced
½ teaspoon dried thyme

CHICKEN
2 pounds boneless skinless chicken breast halves
⅓ cup liquid smoke
1½ cups hickory smoke-flavored barbecue sauce
16 slider buns or dinner rolls, split and warmed

1. In a large bowl, mix brine ingredients, stirring to dissolve brown sugar. Reserve 1 cup brine for cooking chicken; cover and refrigerate.

2. Place chicken in a large resealable bag; add remaining brine. Seal bag, pressing out as much air as possible; turn to coat chicken. Place in a large bowl; refrigerate 18-24 hours, turning occasionally.

3. Remove the chicken from brine and transfer to a 3-qt. slow cooker; discard brine in bag. Add reserved 1 cup brine and ⅓ cup liquid smoke to the chicken. Cook, covered, on low 4-5 hours or until chicken is tender.

4. Remove chicken; cool slightly. Discard cooking juices. Shred chicken with two forks and return to slow cooker. Stir in the barbecue sauce; heat through. Serve on buns.

DID YOU KNOW?

Brining means to soak meat in a solution of water and salt. A brine can be flavored with sugars, juices or seasonings. Kosher salt, table salt or even sea salt can be used in a brining solution. The brining process is a way to help tenderize lean meats such as poultry—or fish or seafood—because lean meats can easily dry out during the cooking process.

Cranberry BBQ Pulled Pork

Tangy cranberry sauce takes traditional pulled pork to a whole new level. My family can't get enough of it! The meat cooks to tender perfection in the slow cooker and is easy to bring to parties, too.

—**CARRIE WIEGAND** MT. PLEASANT, IA

PREP: 20 MIN. • **COOK:** 9 HOURS
MAKES: 14 SERVINGS

1 boneless pork shoulder roast
  (4 to 6 pounds)
1/3 cup cranberry juice
1 teaspoon salt

SAUCE

1 can (14 ounces) whole-berry
  cranberry sauce
1 cup ketchup
1/3 cup cranberry juice
3 tablespoons brown sugar
4 1/2 teaspoons chili powder
2 teaspoons garlic powder
1 teaspoon onion powder
1/2 teaspoon salt
1/4 teaspoon ground chipotle pepper
1/2 teaspoon liquid smoke, optional
14 hamburger buns, split

1. Cut pork roast in half. Place in a 4-qt. slow cooker. Add cranberry juice and salt. Cover and cook on low for 8-10 hours or until meat is tender.

2. Remove the pork roast and set aside. In a small saucepan, combine cranberry sauce, ketchup, cranberry juice, brown sugar, seasonings and liquid smoke if desired. Cook and stir over medium heat for 5 minutes or until slightly thickened.

3. Skim fat from cooking juices; set aside 1/2 cup juices. Discard remaining juices. When cool enough to handle, shred pork with two forks and return to slow cooker.

4. Stir in the sauce mixture and reserved cooking juices. Cover and cook on low for 1 hour or until heated through. Serve on hamburger buns.

DID YOU KNOW?

Originating around Mexico City, chipotles are smoked and dried jalapeno peppers. Chipotles have a medium to hot heat level and are used in a variety of Mexican and American dishes.

Slow-Cooked Reuben Brats

Sauerkraut gives these beer-simmered bratwursts an amazing boost of flavor, but I think it's the special chili sauce that puts them over the top. You may want to make an extra batch of sauce to put on burgers, too—it's that good!

—ALANA SIMMONS JOHNSTOWN, PA

PREP: 30 MIN. • **COOK:** 7¼ HOURS
MAKES: 10 SERVINGS

- 10 uncooked bratwurst links
- 3 cans (12 ounces each) light beer or nonalcoholic beer
- 1 large sweet onion, sliced
- 1 can (14 ounces) sauerkraut, rinsed and well drained
- ¾ cup mayonnaise
- ¼ cup chili sauce
- 2 tablespoons ketchup
- 1 tablespoon finely chopped onion
- 2 teaspoons sweet pickle relish
- 1 garlic clove, minced
- ⅛ teaspoon pepper
- 10 hoagie buns, split
- 10 slices Swiss cheese

1. In a large skillet, brown bratwurst in batches; drain. In a 5-qt. slow cooker, combine beer, sliced onion and sauerkraut; top with bratwurst. Cook, covered, on low 7-9 hours or until sausages are cooked through.

2. Preheat oven to 350°. In a small bowl, mix mayonnaise, chili sauce, ketchup, chopped onion, pickle relish, garlic and pepper until blended. Spread over cut sides of buns; top with cheese, bratwurst and sauerkraut mixture. Place on an ungreased baking sheet. Bake 8-10 minutes or until cheese is melted.

Fabulous Fajitas, p. 124

CHAPTER 5

BEEF ENTREES

Satisfy even the biggest appetites with meaty main dishes.

Meat Loaf with Chili Sauce

When I had a restaurant, this saucy meat loaf was a specialty and one of the most popular items on the menu. I adapted the recipe to go in my slow cooker at home.

—ROBERT COX LAS CRUCES, NM

PREP: 20 MIN.
COOK: 3 HOURS + STANDING
MAKES: 8 SERVINGS

  1   large onion, finely chopped
 ½   cup seasoned bread crumbs
  1   small green pepper, chopped
  2   eggs, lightly beaten
 ½   cup chili sauce
  2   tablespoons spicy brown mustard
  3   to 4 garlic cloves, minced
 ¾   teaspoon salt
 ¼   teaspoon dried oregano
 ¼   teaspoon dried basil
  2   pounds lean ground beef (90% lean)
       Additional chili sauce, optional

1. Cut four 20x3-in. strips of heavy-duty foil; crisscross the strips in the center so they resemble the spokes of a wheel. Place the strips on the bottom and up the sides of a 5-qt. slow cooker. Coat strips with cooking spray.

2. In a large bowl, combine the first 10 ingredients. Add beef; mix lightly but thoroughly. Shape mixture into a 9-in. round loaf. Place loaf in center of strips in slow cooker.

3. Cook, covered, on low 3-4 hours or until a thermometer reads at least 160°. If desired, spoon additional chili sauce over the meat loaf; let stand 10 minutes. Using the foil strips as handles, remove meat loaf to a platter.

FREEZE OPTION Securely wrap and freeze cooled meat loaf in plastic wrap and foil. To use, partially thaw in refrigerator overnight. Unwrap meat loaf; reheat on a greased shallow baking pan in a preheated 350° oven until heated through and a thermometer inserted in center reads 165°.

TOP TIP

Meat loaves and layered dishes are easier to remove from a slow cooker when you create handles using strips of heavy-duty aluminum foil. The ends of the foil strips should drape over the top edge of the slow cooker for easy grasping later. Be sure to coat the strips with enough cooking spray to prevent the meat loaf or other food from sticking to the foil.

Slow Cooker Pot Roast

I work full-time but love fixing home-cooked meals for my husband and son. It's a treat to walk in the door and smell a simmering roast I know will be fall-apart tender and delicious.

—GINA JACKSON OGDENSBURG, NY

PREP: 15 MIN. • **COOK:** 6 HOURS
MAKES: 6 SERVINGS

1   cup warm water
1   tablespoon beef base
½   pound sliced fresh mushrooms
1   large onion, coarsely chopped
3   garlic cloves, minced
1   boneless beef chuck roast (3 pounds)
½   teaspoon pepper
1   tablespoon Worcestershire sauce
¼   cup butter, cubed
⅓   cup all-purpose flour
¼   teaspoon salt

1. In a 5- or 6-qt. slow cooker, whisk the water and beef base; add the mushrooms, onion and garlic. Sprinkle the roast with pepper; transfer to slow cooker. Drizzle with Worcestershire. Cook, covered, on low 6-8 hours or until meat is tender.

2. Remove the roast to a serving platter; tent with foil. Strain the cooking juices, reserving vegetables. Skim fat from the cooking juices. In a large saucepan, melt the butter over medium heat. Stir in flour and salt until smooth; gradually whisk in the cooking juices. Bring to a boil, stirring constantly; cook and stir 1-2 minutes or until thickened. Stir in cooked vegetables. Serve with roast.

NOTE Look for beef base near the broth and bouillon.

DID YOU KNOW?

Worcestershire sauce, which is generally made of soy sauce, vinegar, garlic, molasses, tamarind, onions and various seasonings, was originally considered a mistake. In 1835, English Lord Sandys commissioned two chemists from Worcestershire, John Lea and William Perrins, to duplicate a sauce he had acquired in India. The pungent batch proved disappointing and ended up in the cellar. When the pair stumbled upon the sauce 2 years later, they tasted it and were pleasantly surprised.

Barbecue Beef Brisket

Brisket is such a simple dish, but it's so good when slow-cooked to perfection. Pair the sliced beef with homemade mashed potatoes to soak up every drop of savory gravy.
—*TASTE OF HOME* TEST KITCHEN

PREP: 20 MIN. • **COOK:** 6 HOURS
MAKES: 6 SERVINGS

- 1   fresh beef brisket (3 pounds)
- 1   cup barbecue sauce
- 1/2   cup finely chopped onion
- 2   tablespoons Worcestershire sauce
- 1   tablespoon prepared horseradish
- 1   teaspoon salt
- 1/2   teaspoon pepper
- 3   tablespoons cornstarch
- 1/4   cup cold water

1. Cut the brisket in half; place in a 5-qt. slow cooker. Combine the barbecue sauce, onion, Worcestershire sauce, horseradish, salt and pepper; pour over the beef. Cover and cook on low for 6-7 hours or until the meat is tender.

2. Remove beef and keep warm. Transfer cooking juices to a large saucepan; bring to a boil. Combine cornstarch and water until smooth. Gradually stir into pan. Bring to a boil; cook and stir for 2 minutes or until thickened. Slice meat across the grain; serve with gravy.

NOTE This is a fresh beef brisket, not corned beef.

Beef & Rice Stuffed Cabbage Rolls

My family rushes to the table when I serve my cabbage rolls. The little stuffed bundles go neatly into the slow cooker and always turn out perfectly. To make them a bit healthier, I use brown rice and lean ground beef.

—**LYNN BOWEN** GERALDINE, AL

PREP: 20 MIN. • **COOK:** 6 HOURS
MAKES: 6 SERVINGS

- 12 cabbage leaves
- 1 cup cooked brown rice
- ¼ cup finely chopped onion
- 1 egg, lightly beaten
- ¼ cup fat-free milk
- ½ teaspoon salt
- ¼ teaspoon pepper
- 1 pound lean ground beef (90% lean)

SAUCE

- 1 can (8 ounces) tomato sauce
- 1 tablespoon brown sugar
- 1 tablespoon lemon juice
- 1 teaspoon Worcestershire sauce

1. In batches, cook the cabbage in boiling water 3-5 minutes or until crisp-tender. Drain; cool slightly. Trim the thick vein from the bottom of each cabbage leaf, making a V-shaped cut.

2. In a large bowl, combine the brown rice, onion, egg, milk, salt and pepper. Add the beef; mix lightly but thoroughly. Place about ¼ cup mixture on each cabbage leaf. Pull together the cut edges of the leaf to overlap; fold over the filling. Fold in the sides and roll up.

3. Place six cabbage rolls in a 4- or 5-qt. slow cooker, seam side down. In a bowl, mix the sauce ingredients; pour half of the sauce over the cabbage rolls. Top with remaining rolls and sauce. Cook, covered, on low 6-8 hours or until a thermometer inserted in the beef reads 160° and the cabbage is tender.

Mexican Beef-Stuffed Peppers

I grew up eating stuffed peppers and thought my husband would like them as much as I do. When he shied away from traditional versions, I decided to spice them up using his favorite south-of-the-border flavors.

—NICOLE SULLIVAN ARVADA, CO

PREP: 15 MIN. • **COOK:** 5 HOURS
MAKES: 4 SERVINGS

- 4 medium green or sweet red peppers
- 1 pound ground beef
- 1 package (8.8 ounces) ready-to-serve Spanish rice
- 2 cups (8 ounces) shredded Colby-Monterey Jack cheese, divided
- 1½ cups salsa
- 1 tablespoon hot pepper sauce
- 1 cup water
- 2 tablespoons minced fresh cilantro

1. Cut the tops off peppers and remove the seeds; set aside. In a large skillet, cook the beef over medium heat until no longer pink; drain.

2. Stir in the rice, 1½ cups cheese, salsa and pepper sauce. Spoon into the peppers. Transfer to a 5-qt. slow cooker. Pour water around peppers.

3. Cover and cook on low for 5-6 hours or until peppers are tender and filling is heated through. Top with remaining cheese; sprinkle with cilantro.

Slow-Cooked Stroganoff

I've been preparing creamy beef Stroganoff in the slow cooker for more than 30 years. Once you've made it this way, you may never want to cook it on the stovetop again!
—**KAREN HERBERT** PLACERVILLE, CA

PREP: 20 MIN. • **COOK:** 5 HOURS
MAKES: 8-10 SERVINGS

---

2   beef top round steaks (about ¾ inch thick and 1½ pounds each)
½   cup all-purpose flour
1½ teaspoons salt
½   teaspoon ground mustard
⅛   teaspoon pepper
1   medium onion, sliced and separated into rings
1   can (8 ounces) mushroom stems and pieces, drained
1   can (10½ ounces) condensed beef broth, undiluted
1½ cups (12 ounces) sour cream
   Hot cooked noodles

1. Cut round steaks into 3x½-in. strips. In a shallow bowl, mix flour, salt, mustard and pepper. Add beef in batches; toss to coat.

2. In a 5-qt. slow cooker, layer the onion, mushrooms and beef. Pour broth over top. Cook, covered, on low 5-7 hours or until meat is tender. Just before serving, stir in the sour cream. Serve with noodles.

Spinach & Feta Stuffed Flank Steak

Loaded with a cheese-and-veggie stuffing, these flank steak spirals have an upscale feel that makes them special enough for guests. The accompanying gravy is wonderful over a side of noodles or potatoes.

—**STEVEN SCHEND** GRAND RAPIDS, MI

PREP: 30 MIN. • **COOK:** 6 HOURS
MAKES: 6 SERVINGS

1	beef flank steak (1½ pounds)
2	cups (8 ounces) crumbled feta cheese
3	cups fresh baby spinach
½	cup oil-packed sun-dried tomatoes, drained and chopped
½	cup finely chopped onion
5	tablespoons all-purpose flour, divided
½	teaspoon salt
½	teaspoon pepper
2	tablespoons canola oil
1	cup beef broth
1	tablespoon Worcestershire sauce
2	teaspoons tomato paste
⅓	cup dry red wine or additional beef broth
	Hot cooked egg noodles, optional

1. Starting at one long side, cut the steak horizontally in half to within ½ in. of opposite side. Open steak flat; cover with plastic wrap. Pound with a meat mallet to ½-in. thickness. Remove plastic.

2. Sprinkle 1 cup cheese over the steak to within 1 in. of the edges. Layer with spinach, sun-dried tomatoes, onion and remaining cheese. Roll up jelly-roll style, starting with a long side; tie at 1½-in. intervals with kitchen string. Sprinkle with 2 tablespoons flour, salt and pepper.

3. In a large skillet, heat oil over medium heat. Brown the beef on all sides; drain. Transfer to a 6-qt. oval slow cooker. In a small bowl, mix broth, Worcestershire sauce and tomato paste; pour over top. Cook, covered, on low 6-8 hours or until meat is tender.

4. Remove beef to a platter; keep warm. Transfer the cooking juices to a small saucepan; skim fat. Bring juices to a boil. Mix the remaining flour and wine until smooth; gradually stir into pan. Return to a boil; cook and stir 1-2 minutes or until thickened. Serve beef with gravy and, if desired, noodles.

Super Short Ribs

The name of this recipe says it all! My mother used to prepare these amazing short ribs in the oven. I tried adapting them for the slow cooker and was really happy with the results. For a finishing touch, sprinkle on a little minced fresh parsely before serving.

—**COLEEN CARTER** MALONE, NY

PREP: 20 MIN. • **COOK:** 8 HOURS
MAKES: 6 SERVINGS

3	medium onions, cut into wedges
3	to 3½ pounds bone-in beef short ribs
1	bay leaf
1	bottle (12 ounces) light beer or nonalcoholic beer
2	tablespoons brown sugar
2	tablespoons Dijon mustard
2	tablespoons tomato paste
2	teaspoons dried thyme
2	teaspoons beef bouillon granules
1	teaspoon salt
¼	teaspoon pepper
3	tablespoons all-purpose flour
½	cup cold water
	Hot cooked noodles

1. Place the onions in a 5-qt. slow cooker; add ribs and bay leaf. Combine the beer, brown sugar, mustard, tomato paste, thyme, bouillon, salt and pepper. Pour over meat.

2. Cover and cook on low for 8-10 hours or until meat is tender.

3. Remove the meat and vegetables to a serving platter; keep warm. Discard the bay leaf. Skim fat from the cooking juices; transfer juices to a small saucepan. Bring liquid to a boil.

4. Combine flour and water until smooth. Gradually stir into the pan. Bring to a boil; cook and stir for 2 minutes or until thickened. Serve with meat and noodles.

TOP TIP

To freeze leftover tomato paste, line a baking sheet with waxed paper. Mound the tomato paste in 1-tablespoon portions on the waxed paper. Freeze them until firm, then transfer them to a resealable freezer bag.

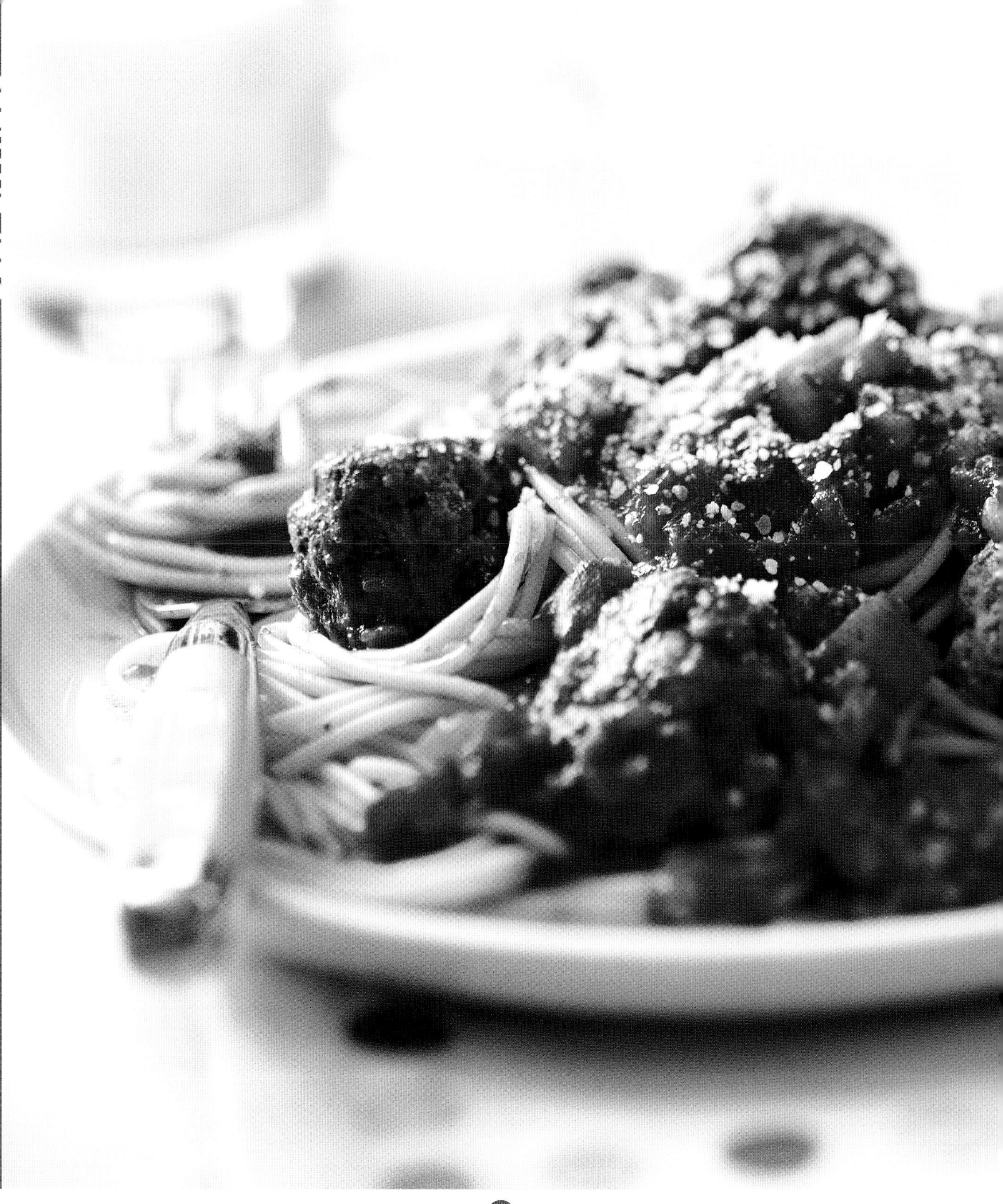

Slow-Cooked Spaghetti & Meatballs

After I tasted my sister-in-law's terrific spaghetti and meatballs, it became a mainstay on my own menus. The large yield means it's a great choice for potluck dinners, too.

—JACKIE GRANT VANDERHOOF, BC

PREP: 20 MIN. • **COOK:** 8 HOURS
MAKES: 20 SERVINGS (ABOUT 4½ QUARTS)

1   cup finely chopped onion, divided
1   teaspoon salt
½   teaspoon pepper
3   pounds ground beef
1   can (46 ounces) tomato juice
1   can (28 ounces) diced tomatoes, drained
1   can (15 ounces) tomato sauce
2   celery ribs, chopped
3   bay leaves
2   garlic cloves, minced
    Hot cooked spaghetti

1. In a large bowl, combine ½ cup onion, salt and pepper. Crumble beef over mixture and mix well. Shape into 1-in. balls. In a large skillet over medium heat, brown meatballs with remaining onion.

2. Transfer to a 5-qt. slow cooker; add the tomato juice, tomatoes, tomato sauce, celery, bay leaves and garlic. Cover and cook on low for 8-10 hours or until heated through, stirring occasionally. Discard the bay leaves. Serve with spaghetti.

Garlic-Sesame Beef

A neighbor introduced my mother to this marinade when she was living in Seoul, South Korea, which is where I was adopted. Mom used to celebrate "heritage night" for my brother and me by serving Korean bulgogi with sticky rice, kimchi and chopsticks. Today I'm a busy mother of four, but I keep her food traditions alive with the help of my slow cooker.

—JACKIE BROWN FAIRVIEW, NC

PREP: 15 MIN. + MARINATING • **COOK:** 5 HOURS
MAKES: 6 SERVINGS

- 6 green onions, sliced
- ½ cup sugar
- ½ cup water
- ½ cup reduced-sodium soy sauce
- ¼ cup sesame oil
- 3 tablespoons sesame seeds, toasted
- 2 tablespoons all-purpose flour
- 4 garlic cloves, minced
- 1 beef sirloin tip roast (3 pounds), thinly sliced
  Additional sliced green onions and toasted sesame seeds
  Hot cooked rice

1. In a large resealable plastic bag, mix the first eight ingredients. Add the beef; seal the bag and turn to coat. Refrigerate 8 hours or overnight.

2. Pour the beef and marinade into a 3-qt. slow cooker. Cook, covered, on low 5-7 hours or until meat is tender.

3. Using a slotted spoon, remove beef to a serving platter; sprinkle with additional green onions and sesame seeds. Serve with rice.

Slow Cooker Pizza Casserole

When it comes to crowd-pleasing food, a saucy pizza casserole with lots of pasta, pepperoni and cheese is hard to beat.
—**VIRGINIA KRITES** CRIDERSVILLE, OH

PREP: 20 MIN. • **COOK:** 2 HOURS
MAKES: 12-14 SERVINGS

1	package (16 ounces) rigatoni or large tube pasta
1½	pounds ground beef
1	small onion, chopped
4	cups (16 ounces) shredded part-skim mozzarella cheese
2	cans (15 ounces each) pizza sauce
1	can (10¾ ounces) condensed cream of mushroom soup, undiluted
1	package (8 ounces) sliced pepperoni

1. Cook pasta according to package directions. Meanwhile, in a skillet, cook beef and onion over medium heat until meat is no longer pink; drain.

2. Drain pasta; place in a 5-qt. slow cooker. Stir in the beef mixture, cheese, pizza sauce, soup and pepperoni. Cover and cook on low for 2-3 hours or until heated through.

DID YOU KNOW?

While some cooks add oil to the water to prevent pasta from sticking together while cooking, others skip this step to avoid any oily residue that can cause sauce to slide off the pasta. The *Taste of Home* Test Kitchen cooks prefer not to add oil to the water.

Fabulous Fajitas

I've enjoyed cooking since I was a young girl growing up in the Southwest. When friends ask me for new recipes to try, I often suggest these flavorful fajitas. Pile on toppings such as shredded cheddar cheese, salsa and sour cream for a fantastic dinner.

—**JANIE REITZ** ROCHESTER, MN

PREP: 20 MIN. • **COOK:** 3½ HOURS
MAKES: 6-8 SERVINGS

1½ pounds beef top sirloin steak, cut into thin strips
2 tablespoons canola oil
2 tablespoons lemon juice
1 garlic clove, minced
1½ teaspoons ground cumin
1 teaspoon seasoned salt
½ teaspoon chili powder
¼ to ½ teaspoon crushed red pepper flakes
1 large green pepper, julienned
1 large onion, julienned
6 to 8 flour tortillas (8 inches)
Shredded cheddar cheese, salsa, sour cream, lettuce and tomatoes, optional

1. In a large skillet, brown the steak strips in oil over medium heat. Place the steak and drippings in a 3-qt. slow cooker. Stir in the lemon juice, garlic, cumin, salt, chili powder and red pepper flakes.

2. Cover and cook on high for 2-3 hours or until the meat is almost tender. Add the green pepper and onion; cover and cook for 1 hour or until the meat and vegetables are tender.

3. Warm the flour tortillas according to the package directions; spoon the beef and vegetables down the center of the tortillas. Top each with shredded cheddar cheese, salsa, sour cream, lettuce and tomatoes if desired.

TOP TIP

Fajitas and stir-frys often call for slicing raw meat into thin strips, which can be difficult to do. To make the meat firmer so it is easier to slice, partially freeze it before slicing. It takes about 30 minutes in the freezer to partially freeze thin cuts of meat.

Stuffed Turkey with Mojo Sauce, p. 151

CHAPTER 6

POULTRY ENTREES

These chicken and turkey specialties are guaranteed to please.

Sweet-and-Sour Chicken

Enjoy a restaurant-worthy Asian dish straight from the slow cooker. Adding the pineapple, onions and snow peas later in the process keeps them from becoming overcooked.
—**DOROTHY HESS** HARTWELL, GA

PREP: 15 MIN. • **COOK:** 3 HOURS 20 MIN.
MAKES: 5 SERVINGS

1¼ pounds boneless skinless chicken breasts, cut into 1-inch strips
  1 tablespoon canola oil
     Salt and pepper to taste
  1 can (8 ounces) pineapple chunks
  1 can (8 ounces) sliced water chestnuts, drained
  2 medium carrots, sliced
  2 tablespoons soy sauce
  4 teaspoons cornstarch
  1 cup sweet-and-sour sauce
  1 cup water
  1 teaspoons ground ginger
     green onions, cut into 1-inch pieces
     cups fresh or frozen snow peas
     Hot cooked rice

1. In a large skillet, saute chicken in oil for 4-5 minutes; drain. Sprinkle with salt and pepper. Drain pineapple, reserving juice; set pineapple aside. In a 5-qt. slow cooker, combine the chicken, water chestnuts, carrots, soy sauce and pineapple juice. Cover and cook on low for 3 hours or until chicken juices run clear.

2. In a small bowl, combine the cornstarch, sweet-and-sour sauce, water and ginger until smooth. Stir into the slow cooker. Add the onions and reserved pineapple; cover and cook on high for 15 minutes or until thickened. Add peas; cook 5 minutes longer. Serve with rice.

DID YOU KNOW?

Snow peas are sweet, tender peas in an edible pod and are eaten whole. They have smaller peas and more translucent pods than the sugar snap variety. Fresh snow peas are available year-round. Select snow peas that are flat, about 3 inches long, light green and shiny.

Herbed Turkey Breasts

Tender, moist turkey is enhanced with a flavorful marinade in this recipe. It's a great option for a holiday dinner.
—**LAURIE MACE** LOS OSOS, CA

PREP: 25 MIN. + MARINATING • **COOK:** 3½ HOURS
MAKES: 12 SERVINGS

1	can (14½ ounces) chicken broth
½	cup lemon juice
¼	cup packed brown sugar
¼	cup fresh sage
¼	cup fresh thyme leaves
¼	cup lime juice
¼	cup cider vinegar
¼	cup olive oil
1	envelope onion soup mix
2	tablespoons Dijon mustard
1	tablespoon minced fresh marjoram
1½	teaspoons paprika
1	teaspoon garlic powder
1	teaspoon pepper
½	teaspoon salt
2	boneless skinless turkey breast halves (2 pounds each)

1. In a blender, process the first 15 ingredients until blended. Pour marinade into a large resealable plastic bag; add the turkey. Seal bag and turn to coat; refrigerate for 8 hours or overnight.

2. Transfer turkey and marinade to a 5-qt. slow cooker. Cover and cook on high for 3½ to 4½ hours or until a thermometer reads 165°.

Ham & Swiss Chicken Roll-Ups

White wine dresses up canned cream soup to make a lovely sauce for roll-ups of chicken, ham and cheese. This tried-and-true recipe comes from my mother.

—**CAROL McCOLLOUGH** MISSOULA, MT

PREP: 25 MIN. + CHILLING
COOK: 4 HOURS • **MAKES:** 6 SERVINGS

- 6 **boneless skinless chicken breast halves (4 ounces each)**
- 6 **thin slices deli ham**
- 6 **slices Swiss cheese**
- 1/4 **cup all-purpose flour**
- 1/4 **cup grated Parmesan cheese**
- 1/2 **teaspoon salt**
- 1/4 **teaspoon pepper**
- 2 **tablespoons canola oil**
- 1 **can (10¾ ounces) condensed cream of chicken soup, undiluted**
- 1/2 **cup dry white wine or chicken broth Hot cooked rice**

1. Flatten chicken to ¼-in. thickness. Top each piece with a slice of ham and Swiss cheese. Roll up tightly; secure with toothpicks. In a shallow bowl, combine the flour, Parmesan cheese, salt and pepper. Roll the chicken in the flour mixture; refrigerate for 1 hour.

2. In a large skillet, brown the roll-ups in oil on all sides; transfer to a 3-qt. slow cooker. Combine the soup and wine or broth; pour over chicken.

3. Cover and cook on low for 4-5 hours or until meat is no longer pink. Remove the roll-ups and stir the sauce. Discard the toothpicks. Serve with rice.

FREEZE OPTION Freeze the cooled chicken roll-ups and sauce in freezer containers. To use, partially thaw in refrigerator overnight. Heat through in a covered saucepan, gently stirring and adding a little broth or milk if necessary.

HOW TO

FLATTEN CHICKEN BREASTS

❶ Place chicken breasts between two pieces of waxed paper on a cutting board.

❷ Using the flat side of a meat mallet, a rolling pin or a soup can, gently pound the chicken evenly to ¼ inch or the desired thickness. Make sure to discard the waxed paper and sanitize all surfaces afterward.

Easy Chicken Tamale Pie

Some basic ingredients from the pantry are all you need to fix this zesty Mexican pie.
—**PETER HALFERTY** CORPUS CHRISTI, TX

PREP: 20 MIN. • **COOK:** 7 HOURS
MAKES: 8 SERVINGS

- 1 pound ground chicken
- 1 teaspoon ground cumin
- 1 teaspoon chili powder
- 1/2 teaspoon salt
- 1/4 teaspoon pepper
- 1 can (15 ounces) black beans, rinsed and drained
- 1 can (14 1/2 ounces) diced tomatoes, undrained
- 1 can (11 ounces) whole kernel corn, drained
- 1 can (10 ounces) enchilada sauce
- 2 green onions, chopped
- 1/4 cup minced fresh cilantro
- 1 package (8 1/2 ounces) corn bread/muffin mix
- 2 eggs, lightly beaten
- 1 cup (4 ounces) shredded Mexican cheese blend
  Optional toppings: sour cream, salsa and minced fresh cilantro

1. In a large skillet, cook ground chicken over medium heat 6-8 minutes or until no longer pink, breaking into crumbles. Stir in seasonings.

2. Transfer to a 4-qt. slow cooker. Stir in beans, tomatoes, corn, enchilada sauce, green onions and cilantro. Cook, covered, on low 6-8 hours or until heated through.

3. In a small bowl, combine muffin mix and eggs; spoon over chicken mixture. Cook, covered, on low 1 to 1 1/2 hours longer or until a toothpick inserted in the corn bread layer comes out clean.

4. Sprinkle with cheese; let stand, covered, 5 minutes. If desired, serve with toppings.

TOP TIP

Like other fresh herbs, cilantro (also known as Chinese parsley) should be used as soon as possible for best results. For short-term storage, immerse freshly cut cilantro stems in water about 2 inches deep. Cover the leaves loosely with a plastic bag and refrigerate for several days. Wash just before using.

Chicken Corn Bread Casserole

I love this slow-cooker casserole! Even though it uses shredded cooked chicken, the taste reminds me of Thanksgiving dinner. With chunks of corn bread and vegetables, it makes such a comforting meal on a chilly fall or winter evening.
—**NANCY BARKER** PEORIA, AZ

PREP: 40 MIN. • **COOK:** 3 HOURS
MAKES: 6 SERVINGS

- 5 cups cubed corn bread
- ¼ cup butter, cubed
- 1 large onion, chopped (about 2 cups)
- 4 celery ribs, chopped (about 2 cups)
- 3 cups shredded cooked chicken
- 1 can (10¾ ounces) condensed cream of chicken soup, undiluted
- 1 can (10¾ ounces) condensed cream of mushroom soup, undiluted
- ½ cup reduced-sodium chicken broth
- 1 teaspoon poultry seasoning
- ½ teaspoon salt
- ½ teaspoon rubbed sage
- ¼ teaspoon pepper

1. Preheat oven to 350°. Place the corn bread cubes on an ungreased 15x10x1-in. baking pan. Bake 20-25 minutes or until toasted. Cool on baking pan.

2. In a large skillet, heat butter over medium-high heat. Add onion and celery; cook and stir 6-8 minutes or until tender. Transfer to a greased 4-qt. slow cooker. Stir in the corn bread, chicken, soups, broth and seasonings.

3. Cook, covered, on low 3-4 hours or until heated through.

Chicken Cacciatore

Craving Italian? Skip driving to a pricey restaurant and get this saucy seasoned chicken going in the afternoon. By dinnertime, you'll have an extra-special entree to serve over pasta.

—AGGIE ARNOLD-NORMAN LIBERTY, PA

PREP: 15 MIN. • **COOK:** 6 HOURS
MAKES: 6 SERVINGS

- 2 medium onions, thinly sliced
- 1 broiler/fryer chicken (3 to 4 pounds), cut up and skin removed
- 2 garlic cloves, minced
- 1 to 2 teaspoons dried oregano
- 1 teaspoon salt
- ½ teaspoon dried basil
- ¼ teaspoon pepper
- 1 bay leaf
- 1 can (14½ ounces) diced tomatoes, undrained
- 1 can (8 ounces) tomato sauce
- 1 can (4 ounces) mushroom stems and pieces, drained or 1 cup sliced fresh mushrooms
- ¼ cup white wine or water
  Hot cooked pasta

1. Place the onions in a 5-qt. slow cooker. Add chicken, seasonings, tomatoes, tomato sauce, mushrooms and white wine.

2. Cover and cook on low for 6-8 hours or until chicken is tender. Discard the bay leaf. Serve chicken with sauce over pasta.

Slow Cooker Chicken Dinner

Juicy chicken, tender potatoes, carrots and gravy—what more do you need for dinner? It requires only 10 minutes of prep and is ready to enjoy when I get home from the office.

—JENET CATTAR NEPTUNE BEACH, FL

PREP: 10 MIN. • **COOK:** 8 HOURS
MAKES: 4 SERVINGS

- 6 medium red potatoes, cut into chunks
- 4 medium carrots, cut into $\frac{1}{2}$-inch pieces
- 4 boneless skinless chicken breast halves
- 1 can ($10\frac{3}{4}$ ounces) condensed cream of chicken soup, undiluted
- 1 can ($10\frac{3}{4}$ ounces) condensed cream of mushroom soup, undiluted
- $\frac{1}{8}$ teaspoon garlic salt
- 2 to 4 tablespoons mashed potato flakes, optional

1. Place the red potatoes and carrots in a 5-qt. slow cooker. Top with the chicken. Combine the soups and garlic salt; pour over chicken.

2. Cover and cook on low for 8 hours or until the meat and vegetables are tender. To thicken, stir potato flakes into the gravy and cook 30 minutes longer, if desired.

Mandarin Turkey Tenderloin

My husband grew up near farms that raised turkeys, so he learned early on to love dishes featuring that meat. This easy recipe gives it a delicious Asian-style twist.

—LORIE MINER KAMAS, UT

PREP: 15 MIN. • **COOK:** 4½ HOURS
MAKES: 8 SERVINGS

- 8 turkey breast tenderloins (4 ounces each)
- ½ teaspoon ground ginger
- ½ teaspoon crushed red pepper flakes
- 1 can (11 ounces) mandarin oranges, drained
- 1 cup sesame ginger marinade
- ½ cup chicken broth
- 1 package (16 ounces) frozen stir-fry vegetable blend, thawed
- 1 tablespoon sesame seeds, toasted
- 1 green onion, sliced
  Hot cooked rice, optional

1. Place the turkey in a 3-qt. slow cooker. Sprinkle with the ginger and red pepper flakes. Top with the mandarin oranges. In a small bowl, combine the sesame ginger marinade and broth; pour over the turkey. Cover and cook on low for 4-5 hours or until a meat thermometer reads 170°.

2. Stir the vegetables into the slow cooker. Cover and cook 30 minutes longer or until vegetables are heated through.

3. Sprinkle with sesame seeds and green onion. Serve with rice if desired.

FREEZE OPTION Cool the turkey mixture. Freeze in freezer containers. To use, partially thaw in the refrigerator overnight. Heat through slowly in a covered skillet until a thermometer inserted in turkey reads 165°, stirring occasionally and adding a little broth or water if necessary. Garnish as directed.

TOP TIP

Toast sesame seeds in a dry skillet over medium heat for 3-5 minutes or until lightly browned, stirring occasionally. Or bake the seeds on an ungreased baking sheet at 350° for 8-10 minutes or until lightly browned. Be sure to watch to avoid scorching.

Slow-Cooked Turkey Stroganoff

Our family loves turkey, and I've used it in a variety of recipes, but this one is our all-time favorite. I've been fixing the creamy Stroganoff for more than 30 years. To change it up, replace the noodles with mashed potatoes, rice or polenta.

—CINDY ADAMS TRACY, CA

PREP: 20 MIN. • **COOK:** 6 HOURS
MAKES: 6 SERVINGS

4 turkey thighs (about 4 pounds)
1 large onion, halved and thinly sliced
1 can (10¾ ounces) condensed cream of celery soup, undiluted
⅓ cup water
3 garlic cloves, minced
2 teaspoons dried tarragon
½ teaspoon salt
½ teaspoon pepper
½ cup sour cream
Hot cooked egg noodles

1. Place turkey and onion in a 5-qt. slow cooker. In a large bowl, whisk cream of celery soup, water, garlic, tarragon, salt and pepper until blended; pour over the top. Cook, covered, on low 6-8 hours or until meat is tender.

2. Remove turkey from slow cooker. When cool enough to handle, remove meat from bones; discard bones. Shred meat with two forks. Whisk sour cream into the cooking juices; return meat to slow cooker. Serve with noodles.

Mushroom Meat Loaf

I don't consider myself a top-notch cook, but I'm always proud to serve my meat loaf. It's tender and moist, and the sauce has a nice zip to it. The portobello mushrooms go well with the lean ground turkey, too.

—TYLER SHERMAN WILLIAMSBURG, VA

PREP: 30 MIN. • **COOK:** 3¼ HOURS
MAKES: 6 SERVINGS

- 2   eggs, lightly beaten
- 1⅓ cups soft bread crumbs
- ½   pound large portobello mushrooms, stems removed, finely chopped
- 1   small onion, finely chopped
- 2   garlic cloves, minced
- ¾   teaspoon salt
- ½   teaspoon dried thyme
- ¼   teaspoon pepper
- 1   pound lean ground turkey
- ¼   cup chili sauce
- 2   teaspoons stone-ground mustard
- ⅛   teaspoon cayenne pepper

1. Cut three 20x3-in. strips of heavy-duty foil; crisscross the strips so they resemble the spokes of a wheel. Place strips on the bottom and up the sides of a 3-qt. slow cooker. Coat strips with cooking spray.

2. In a large bowl, combine the eggs, bread crumbs, mushrooms, onion, garlic, salt, thyme and pepper. Crumble the turkey over the mixture and mix well. Shape into a 7½x4-in. loaf. Cook immediately or cover and freeze for up to 3 months.

3. Place the meat loaf in the center of the foil strips. Cover and cook on low for 3-4 hours or until no pink remains and a thermometer reads 160°. Combine chili sauce, mustard and cayenne; pour over meat. Cover and cook 15 minutes longer or until heated through. Using foil strips as handles, remove the meat loaf to a platter.

TO USE FROZEN MEAT LOAF Thaw in the refrigerator overnight. Cook as directed.

Peachy Chicken with Sweet Potatoes

When my mom was pregnant with me, home-canned peaches were one of the only things she wanted to eat. To this day, I absolutely love any dish featuring that fruit.
—**SANDRA BONOW** LEWISTON, MN

PREP: 25 MIN. • **COOK:** 6 HOURS
MAKES: 4 SERVINGS

- 2 medium sweet potatoes, peeled and cubed
- 1 medium onion, chopped
- 8 boneless skinless chicken thighs (about 2 pounds)
- 1 teaspoon paprika
- 1 teaspoon dried thyme
- 1/2 teaspoon salt
- 1/8 teaspoon cayenne pepper
- 1 cup peach preserves
- 2 tablespoons cornstarch
- 1/2 cup cold water

1. In a 4- or 5-qt. slow cooker, combine the sweet potatoes and onion. Sprinkle chicken with paprika, thyme, salt and cayenne; arrange over sweet potatoes. Top with preserves. Cover and cook on low for 6-8 hours or until chicken and potatoes are tender.

2. Remove the chicken and vegetables to a serving platter; keep warm. Skim fat from the cooking juices; transfer to a small saucepan. Bring the liquid to a boil. Combine the cornstarch and water until smooth. Gradually stir into the pan. Bring to a boil; cook and stir for 2 minutes or until thickened. Serve with chicken and vegetables.

Stuffed Turkey with Mojo Sauce

A fan of Latin food, I created this dish that blends fresh ingredients and zesty spices.

—MELISSA LAUER SAN ANTONIO, TX

PREP: 30 MIN. • **COOK:** 5 HOURS + STANDING
MAKES: 8 SERVINGS (ABOUT 1 CUP SAUCE)

1   medium green pepper, finely chopped
1   medium onion, finely chopped
2   garlic cloves, minced
2   teaspoons ground coriander
1   teaspoon ground cumin
1/8 teaspoon cayenne pepper
1   pound uncooked chicken sausage links, casings removed
1   fresh boneless turkey breast (4 pounds)
1/4 teaspoon salt
1/4 teaspoon pepper

MOJO SAUCE

1   cup orange juice
1/2 cup fresh cilantro leaves
1/4 cup minced fresh oregano or 4 teaspoons dried oregano
1/4 cup lime juice
4   garlic cloves, minced
1   teaspoon ground cumin
1/2 teaspoon pepper
1/4 teaspoon salt
1/8 teaspoon cayenne pepper
1   cup olive oil

1. In a bowl, combine the first six ingredients. Crumble sausage over mixture and mix well.

2. With the skin side down, pound the turkey breast with meat mallet to 1/2-in. thickness. Sprinkle with salt and pepper. Spread sausage mixture over turkey to within 1 in. of edges. Roll up jelly-roll style, starting with a short side; tie at 1 1/2-in. to 2-in. intervals with kitchen string. Place in a 5-qt. oval slow cooker.

3. In a blender, combine the first nine sauce ingredients. Cover; process until blended. While processing, gradually add the olive oil in a steady stream. Pour over the turkey.

4. Cover and cook on low for 5 hours or until a thermometer inserted in center reads 165°. Remove from slow cooker; cover and let stand for 10 minutes before slicing. Discard string.

5. Meanwhile, skim fat from the cooking juices; transfer juices to a small saucepan. Bring to a boil; cook until the liquid is reduced by half. Serve with turkey.

Ham with Cranberry-Pineapple Sauce, p. 161

CHAPTER 7

PORK & MORE ENTREES

Savor a wide variety, from ham and bacon to shrimp and fish.

Apple-Cinnamon Pork Loin

This comforting roast fills our whole house with the tangy, spicy scents of apples and cinnamon. For a heartwarming supper on a chilly autumn or winter day, I serve the pork with homemade mashed potatoes.
—**RACHEL SCHULTZ** LANSING, MI

PREP: 20 MIN. • **COOK:** 6 HOURS
MAKES: 6 SERVINGS

- 1 boneless pork loin roast (2 to 3 pounds)
- ½ teaspoon salt
- ¼ teaspoon pepper
- 1 tablespoon canola oil
- 3 medium apples, peeled and sliced, divided
- ¼ cup honey
- 1 small red onion, halved and sliced
- 1 tablespoon ground cinnamon
  Minced fresh parsley, optional

1. Sprinkle roast with salt and pepper. In a large skillet, brown roast in oil on all sides; cool slightly. With a paring knife, cut about sixteen 3-in.-deep slits in sides of roast; insert one apple slice into each slit.

2. Place half of the remaining apples in a 4-qt. slow cooker. Place roast over apples. Drizzle with honey; top with onion and remaining apples. Sprinkle with cinnamon.

3. Cover and cook on low for 6-8 hours or until meat is tender. Remove pork and apple mixture; keep warm.

4. Transfer the cooking juices to a small saucepan. Bring to a boil; cook until the liquid is reduced by half. Serve with the pork and apple mixture. Sprinkle with parsley if desired.

Herb Stuffed Chops

I often pass along this slow cooker recipe to newly married couples because I know it will become one of their favorites. Pork chops are an extra-special treat when cut into a pocket and filled with homemade stuffing.
—**DIANA SEEGER** NEW SPRINGFIELD, OH

PREP: 25 MIN. • **COOK:** 8 HOURS
MAKES: 6 SERVINGS

¾ cup chopped onion
¼ cup chopped celery
2 tablespoons butter
2 cups day-old bread cubes
½ cup minced fresh parsley
⅓ cup evaporated milk
1 teaspoon fennel seed, crushed
1½ teaspoons salt, divided
½ teaspoon pepper, divided
6 bone-in pork rib or loin chops
   (8 ounces each)
1 tablespoon canola oil
¾ cup white wine or chicken broth

1. In a small skillet, saute onion and celery in butter until tender. Add the bread cubes, parsley, evaporated milk, fennel, ¼ teaspoon salt and ⅛ teaspoon pepper; toss to coat.

2. Cut a pocket in each chop by slicing from the fat side almost to the bone. Spoon about ¼ cup stuffing into each pocket. Combine the remaining salt and pepper; rub over chops.

3. In a large skillet, brown chops in oil; transfer to a 3-qt. slow cooker. Pour the wine over the top. Cover and cook on low for 8-9 hours or until meat thermometer reads 160°.

HOW TO

MAKE POCKETS IN PORK CHOPS

❶ To form pockets in pork chops for stuffing, use a sharp paring knife to make a horizontal slit in the middle of the fatty side of each chop. Cut from the edge almost to the other side but not through the chop.

❷ Spoon the stuffing mixture into the pockets. If the recipe directs, secure the opening of each pocket with toothpicks.

Cheesy Tater Tots & Canadian Bacon

Family-friendly Tater Tots ensure that kids will like this main dish as much as adults do. It was inspired by Hawaiian-style pizza.
—**LISA RENSHAW** KANSAS CITY, MO

PREP: 15 MIN.
COOK: 4 HOURS + STANDING
MAKES: 8 SERVINGS

- 1 package (32 ounces) frozen Tater Tots, thawed
- 8 ounces Canadian bacon, chopped
- 1 cup frozen pepper strips, thawed and chopped
- 1 medium onion, finely chopped
- 1 can (8 ounces) pineapple tidbits, drained
- 2 eggs
- 3 cans (5 ounces each) evaporated milk
- 1 can (15 ounces) pizza sauce
- 1 cup (4 ounces) shredded provolone cheese
- ½ cup grated Parmesan cheese, optional

1. Place half of the Tater Tots in a greased 5-qt. slow cooker. Layer with Canadian bacon, peppers, onion and pineapple tidbits. Top with remaining Tater Tots. In a large bowl, whisk the eggs, milk and pizza sauce; pour over the top. Sprinkle with provolone cheese.

2. Cook, covered, on low 4-5 hours or until heated through. If desired, sprinkle with Parmesan cheese; let stand, covered, 20 minutes.

TOP TIP

When you need to transport a slow cooker of food to a potluck, consider using a clean laundry basket or heavy-duty storage crate lined with a towel. Take the cover off the slow cooker, put foil over the top and replace the cover. Then place the slow cooker and your serving utensil in the towel-lined basket or crate. Transporting the slow cooker in this way will prevent it from tipping. During the event, put the slow cooker's lid in the basket or crate so you can easily find it later.

Ham with Cranberry-Pineapple Sauce

On hectic holidays, free up your oven for other dishes by preparing your ham in the slow cooker. Pineapple, cranberry sauce and seasonings make a special topping.
—**CAROLE RESNICK** CLEVELAND, OH

PREP: 15 MIN. • **COOK:** 5 HOURS
MAKES: 20 SERVINGS (4½ CUPS SAUCE)

- 1 fully cooked boneless ham (5 to 6 pounds)
- 12 whole cloves
- 1 can (20 ounces) crushed pineapple, undrained
- 1 can (14 ounces) whole-berry cranberry sauce
- 2 garlic cloves, minced
- 2 tablespoons stone-ground mustard
- ½ teaspoon coarsely ground pepper
- 2 tablespoons cornstarch
- 2 tablespoons cold water

1. Score the ham, making ½-in.-deep diamond shapes; insert a whole clove in each diamond. Place the ham in a 5-qt. slow cooker. In a large bowl, combine the pineapple, cranberry sauce, garlic, mustard and pepper; pour over ham.

2. Cover; cook on low for 5-6 hours or until a thermometer reads 140°. Remove meat to a cutting board and keep warm; remove and discard cloves.

3. Transfer sauce to a small saucepan. Bring to a boil. Combine cornstarch and water until smooth; gradually stir into the pan. Bring to a boil; cook and stir for 2 minutes or until thickened. Slice ham and serve with sauce.

TOP TIP

Have extra canned cranberry sauce from the holidays? Take advantage of the leftovers in tasty ways. Stir a few tablespoons into your hot cooked oatmeal. For a delectable dessert, melt the sauce in a saucepan and spoon it over pound cake, angel food cake or ice cream. At lunchtime, spread some sauce on a flour tortilla, layer on sliced cooked turkey and lettuce, then roll it up for an easy wrap.

Pork, Bean & Rice Burritos

The combination of spices is the key to this zippy burrito filling—it's my family's favorite. The mouthwatering aroma that wafts through the air as the pork simmers makes our kitchen smell like a Mexican restaurant.

—**VALONDA SEWARD** COARSEGOLD, CA

PREP: 25 MIN. • **COOK:** 6 HOURS
MAKES: 10 SERVINGS

SPICE RUB

2½ teaspoons garlic powder
2 teaspoons onion powder
1¼ teaspoons salt
1 teaspoon white pepper
1 teaspoon pepper
½ teaspoon ground cumin
½ teaspoon dried oregano
½ teaspoon cayenne pepper

BURRITOS

1 boneless pork shoulder butt roast (3 pounds)
1 cup water
2 tablespoons beef bouillon granules
10 flour tortillas (10 inches)
3 cups canned pinto beans, rinsed and drained
3 cups cooked Spanish rice
Optional toppings: salsa, chopped tomato, shredded lettuce, sour cream, guacamole

1. Mix the spice rub ingredients; rub over pork. Transfer to a 6-qt. slow cooker. In a small bowl, mix water and beef granules; pour around roast. Cook, covered, on low 6-8 hours or until meat is tender.

2. Remove the roast; cool slightly. Reserve ½ cup cooking juices; discard remaining juices. Shred pork with two forks. Return pork and reserved juices to slow cooker; heat through.

3. Spoon a scant ⅓ cup shredded pork across center of each tortilla; top with a scant ⅓ cup each pinto beans and rice. Fold the bottom and sides of the tortilla over the filling and roll up. Serve with toppings as desired.

FREEZE OPTION Cool filling ingredients before making burritos. Individually wrap burritos in paper towels and foil; freeze in a resealable plastic freezer bag. To use, remove foil; place paper towel-wrapped burrito on a microwave-safe plate. Microwave on high for 3-4 minutes or until heated through, turning once. Let stand 20 seconds. Serve with toppings of your choice.

Mushroom Pork Ragout

Bored with the usual pork roast? Bring some excitement to your table with an Italian-style treatment for tenderloin. The slow-cooked meat is so good draped in a tomato sauce and served over egg noodles. Complete the menu with broccoli or green beans on the side and an apple crisp for dessert.

—**CONNIE MCDOWELL** GREENWOOD, DE

PREP: 20 MIN. • **COOK:** 3 HOURS
MAKES: 2 SERVINGS

- 1 pork tenderloin (¾ pound)
- ⅛ teaspoon salt
- ⅛ teaspoon pepper
- 1 tablespoon cornstarch
- ¾ cup canned crushed tomatoes, divided
- 1 tablespoon chopped sun-dried tomatoes (not packed in oil)
- 1¼ teaspoons dried savory
- 1½ cups sliced fresh mushrooms
- ⅓ cup sliced onion
- 1½ cups hot cooked egg noodles

1. Rub the pork tenderloin with the salt and pepper; cut pork tenderloin in half. In a 1½-qt. slow cooker, combine the cornstarch, ½ cup crushed tomatoes, sun-dried tomatoes and savory. Top with mushrooms, onion and pork. Pour the remaining tomatoes over the pork. Cover and cook on low for 3-4 hours or until meat is tender.

2. Remove the pork tenderloin and cut into slices. Stir the cooking juices until smooth; serve with pork and noodles.

DID YOU KNOW?

As the name indicates, sun-dried tomatoes have been dried to remove most of their water content, producing a chewy, intensely flavored tomato product. Sun-dried tomatoes are found in the grocery store either packed in oil or dry-packed. Dry-packed sun-dried tomatoes are sometimes soaked in a liquid to soften them before use in recipes.

Sesame Pork Ribs

These lightly sweet yet tangy ribs are so juicy and flavorful, people think I spent hours doing the prep work. No one ever guesses how easy the recipe actually is to make.
—**SANDY ALEXANDER** FAYETTEVILLE, NC

PREP: 15 MIN. • **COOK:** 5 HOURS
MAKES: 5 SERVINGS

- ¾ cup packed brown sugar
- ½ cup reduced-sodium soy sauce
- ½ cup ketchup
- ¼ cup honey
- 2 tablespoons white wine vinegar
- 3 garlic cloves, minced
- 1 teaspoon salt
- 1 teaspoon ground ginger
- ¼ to ½ teaspoon crushed red pepper flakes
- 5 pounds bone-in country-style pork ribs
- 1 medium onion, sliced
- 2 tablespoons sesame seeds, toasted
- 2 tablespoons chopped green onions

1. In a large bowl, combine the first nine ingredients. Add the ribs and turn to coat. Place the onion in a 5-qt. slow cooker; top with ribs and sauce. Cover and cook on low for 5-6 hours or until meat is tender.

2. Place the ribs on a serving platter; sprinkle with the sesame seeds and green onions.

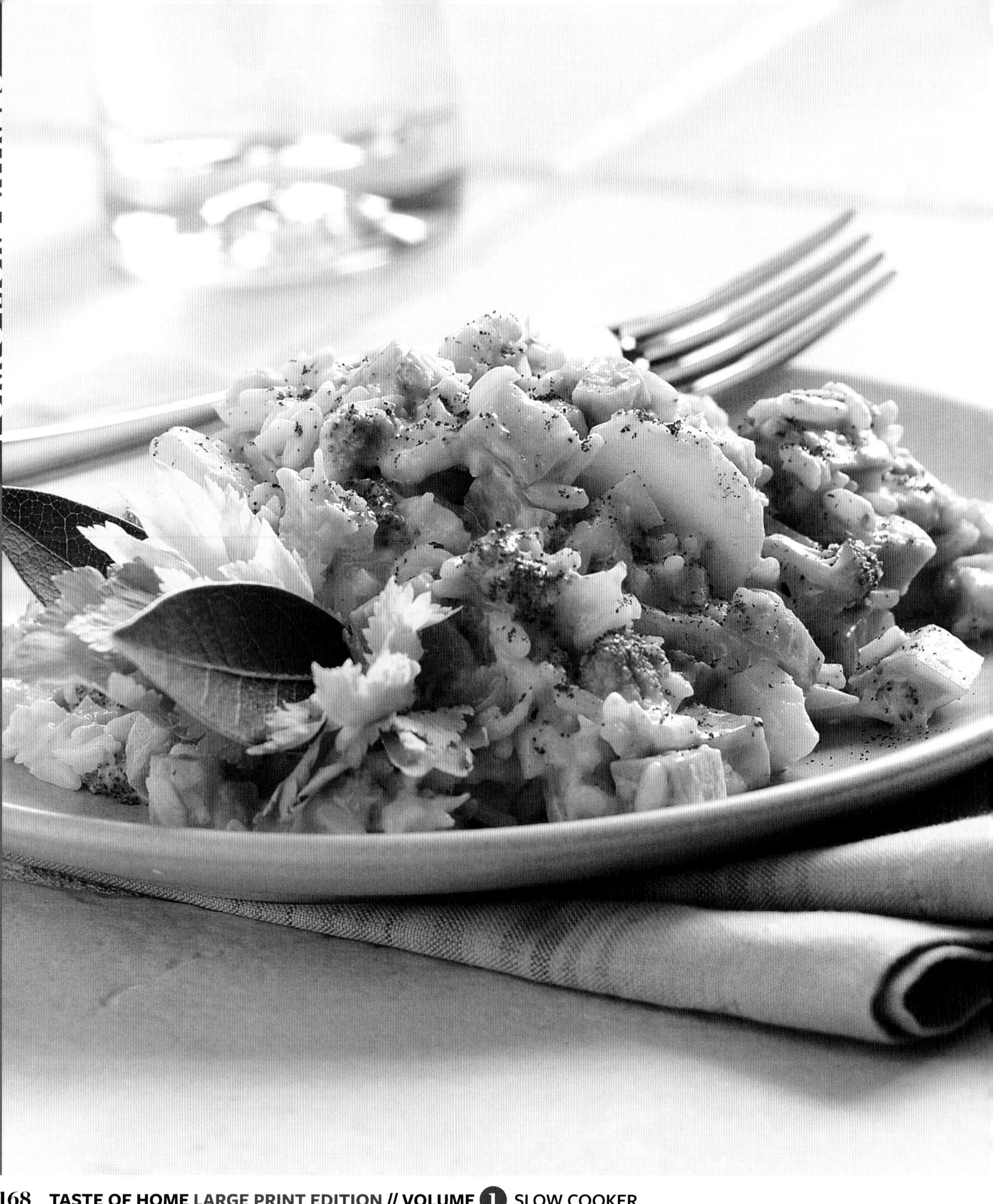

Slow-Cooked Ham 'n' Broccoli

When you don't have time for side dishes, rely on this creamy all-in-one meal that includes rice and vegetables. It's a great way to use up leftover holiday ham, too.

—JILL PENNINGTON JACKSONVILLE, FL

PREP: 10 MIN. • **COOK:** 2 HOURS + STANDING
MAKES: 6-8 SERVINGS

3 cups cubed fully cooked ham
3 cups frozen chopped broccoli, thawed
1 can (10¾ ounces) condensed cream of mushroom soup, undiluted
1 jar (8 ounces) process cheese sauce
1 can (8 ounces) sliced water chestnuts, drained
1¼ cups uncooked instant rice
1 cup 2% milk
1 celery rib, chopped
1 medium onion, chopped
⅛ to ¼ teaspoon pepper
½ teaspoon paprika

In a 3-qt. slow cooker, combine the first 10 ingredients. Cover and cook on high for 2-3 hours or until the rice is tender. Let stand for 10 minutes before serving. Sprinkle with paprika.

Spinach and Sausage Lasagna

Convenient no-cook noodles, frozen spinach and a jar of spaghetti sauce simplify the prep for this Italian classic. It just might become your new go-to recipe for lasagna.
—**KATHY MORROW** HUBBARD, OH

PREP: 25 MIN. • **COOK:** 3 HOURS
MAKES: 8 SERVINGS

- 1 pound bulk Italian sausage
- 1 jar (24 ounces) garden-style spaghetti sauce
- 1/2 cup water
- 1 teaspoon Italian seasoning
- 1/2 teaspoon salt
- 1 carton (15 ounces) ricotta cheese
- 1 package (10 ounces) frozen chopped spinach, thawed and squeezed dry
- 2 cups (8 ounces) shredded part-skim mozzarella cheese, divided
- 9 no-cook lasagna noodles
  Grated Parmesan cheese

1. Cook the sausage in a large skillet over medium heat until no longer pink; drain. Stir in the spaghetti sauce, water, Italian seasoning and salt. Combine the ricotta cheese, spinach and 1 cup mozzarella cheese in a small bowl.

2. Spread 1 cup sauce mixture in a greased oval 5-qt. slow cooker. Layer with three lasagna noodles (breaking the noodles if necessary to fit), 1 1/4 cups sauce mixture and half of the cheese mixture. Repeat layers. Layer with remaining noodles and sauce mixture; sprinkle with remaining mozzarella cheese.

3. Cover and cook on low for 3-4 hours or until noodles are tender. Sprinkle servings with Parmesan cheese.

TOP TIP

Fresh out of Italian seasoning and don't have time for an extra trip to the grocery store? You can blend just a few common kitchen spices as a substitute with good results. Combine 1/4 teaspoon each of basil, thyme, rosemary and oregano for each teaspoon of Italian seasoning called for in a recipe.

Simple Poached Salmon

Here's a fuss-free but delicious way to eat healthy salmon. Enjoy the seasoned fillets warm or cold with lemon wedges.
—**ERIN CHILCOAT** CENTRAL ISLIP, NY

PREP: 10 MIN. • **COOK:** 1½ HOURS
MAKES: 4 SERVINGS

- 2 cups water
- 1 cup white wine
- 1 medium onion, sliced
- 1 celery rib, sliced
- 1 medium carrot, sliced
- 2 tablespoons lemon juice
- 3 fresh thyme sprigs
- 1 fresh rosemary sprig
- 1 bay leaf
- ½ teaspoon salt
- ¼ teaspoon pepper
- 4 salmon fillets (1¼ inches thick and 6 ounces each)
  Lemon wedges

1. In a 3-qt. slow cooker, combine the first 11 ingredients. Cook, covered, on low 45 minutes.

2. Carefully place salmon fillets in the cooking liquid; add additional warm water (120° to 130°) to cover if needed. Cook, covered, 45-55 minutes or just until fish flakes easily with a fork (a thermometer inserted in fish should read at least 145°). Remove fish from cooking liquid. Serve warm or cold with lemon wedges.

Italian Shrimp 'n' Pasta

Italian seasoning adds a twist to this zesty medley of shrimp, chicken, orzo pasta and vegetables. Feel free to replace the orzo with any other small pasta you like.

—**KAREN EDWARDS** SANFORD, ME

PREP: 10 MIN. • **COOK:** 7⅓ HOURS
MAKES: 6-8 SERVINGS

- 1 pound boneless skinless chicken thighs, cut into 2x1-inch strips
- 2 tablespoons canola oil
- 1 can (28 ounces) crushed tomatoes
- 2 celery ribs, chopped
- 1 medium green pepper, cut into 1-inch pieces
- 1 medium onion, coarsely chopped
- 2 garlic cloves, minced
- 1 tablespoon sugar
- ½ teaspoon salt
- ½ teaspoon Italian seasoning
- ⅛ to ¼ teaspoon cayenne pepper
- 1 bay leaf
- ½ cup uncooked orzo pasta or other small pasta
- 1 pound cooked medium shrimp, peeled and deveined

1. In a large skillet, brown the chicken in oil; transfer to a 3-qt. slow cooker. Stir in the next 10 ingredients. Cover and cook on low for 7-8 hours or until the chicken is no longer pink.

2. Discard bay leaf. Stir in pasta; cover and cook on high for 15 minutes or until pasta is tender. Stir in shrimp; cover and cook for 5 minutes longer or until heated through.

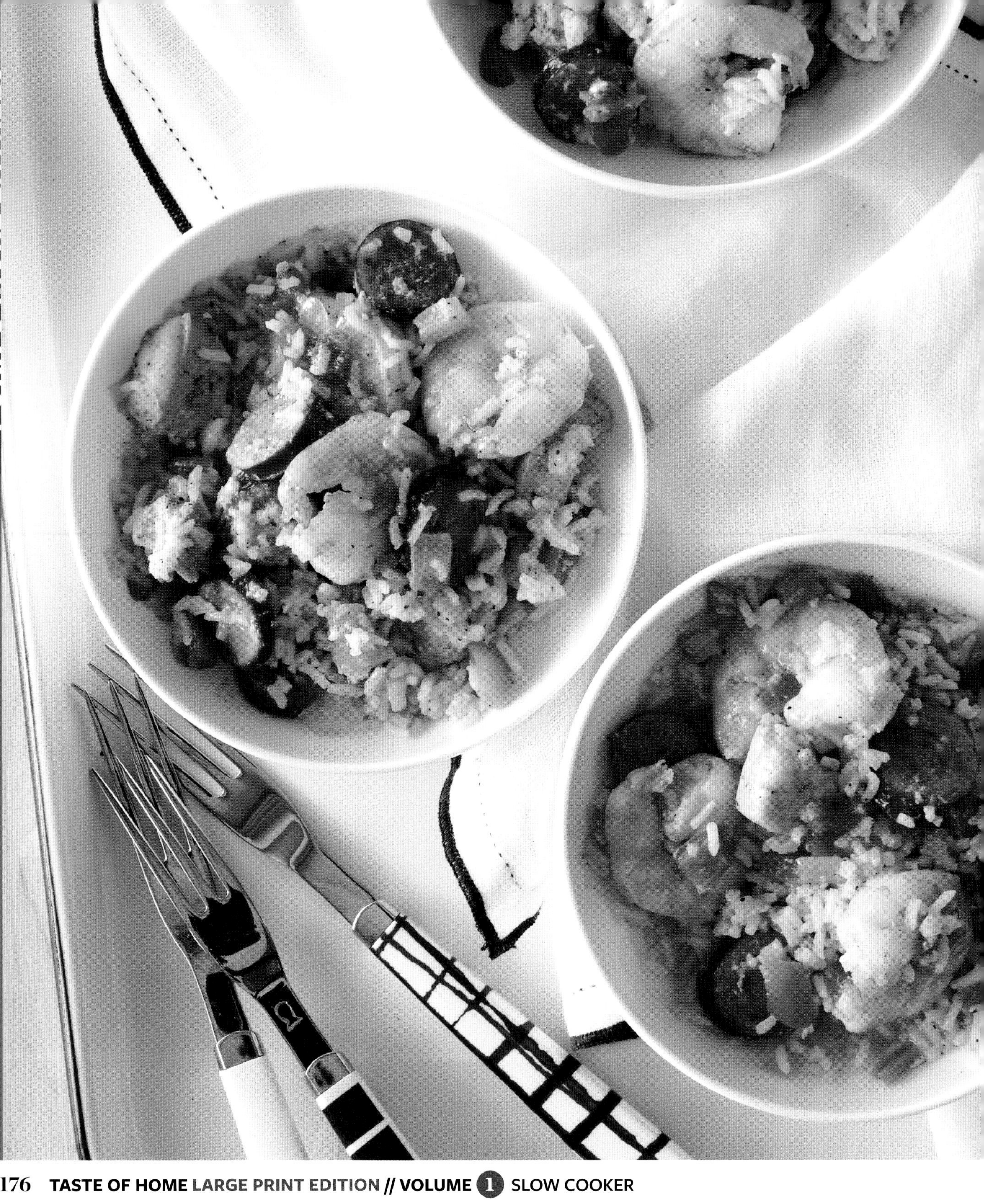

Gulf Coast Jambalaya Rice

As the stew of the South, jambalaya is a much-loved staple. Home cooks have been making their own versions for ages. This slow-cooked variation is my all-time favorite.
—**JUDY BATSON** TAMPA, FL

PREP: 20 MIN. • **COOK:** 3¼ HOURS
MAKES: 8 SERVINGS

1   pound boneless skinless chicken breasts, cut into 1-inch cubes
1   pound smoked kielbasa, cut into ¼-inch slices
2   cups chicken stock
1   large green pepper, chopped
1   cup chopped sweet onion
2   celery ribs, chopped
2   garlic cloves, minced
2   teaspoons Creole seasoning
1   teaspoon seafood seasoning
1   teaspoon pepper
1   pound uncooked medium shrimp, peeled and deveined
2   cups uncooked instant rice

1. Place the first 10 ingredients in a 5-qt. slow cooker. Cook, covered, on low 3-4 hours or until chicken is tender.

2. Stir in shrimp and rice. Cook, covered, 15-20 minutes longer or until shrimp turn pink and rice is tender.

NOTE The following spices may be substituted for 1 teaspoon Creole seasoning: ¼ teaspoon each salt, garlic powder and paprika; and a pinch each of dried thyme, ground cumin and cayenne pepper.

Buffalo Shrimp Mac & Cheese

Love the flavor of Buffalo chicken wings? Then you're sure to enjoy this rich, creamy and slightly spicy dinner. What a great way to change up macaroni and cheese!

—ROBIN HAAS CRANSTON, RI

PREP: 15 MIN. • **COOK:** 3½ HOURS
MAKES: 6 SERVINGS

- 2 cups 2% milk
- 1 cup half-and-half cream
- 2 tablespoons Louisiana-style hot sauce
- 1 tablespoon butter
- 1 teaspoon ground mustard
- ½ teaspoon onion powder
- ¼ teaspoon white pepper
- ¼ teaspoon ground nutmeg
- 2 cups (8 ounces) finely shredded cheddar cheese
- 1 cup (4 ounces) shredded Gouda or Swiss cheese
- 1½ cups uncooked elbow macaroni
- ¾ pound frozen cooked salad shrimp, thawed
- 1 cup (4 ounces) crumbled blue cheese
- 2 tablespoons minced fresh chives
- 2 tablespoons minced fresh parsley
  Additional Louisiana-style hot sauce, optional

1. In a 3-qt. slow cooker, combine the first eight ingredients; stir in shredded cheeses and macaroni. Cook, covered, on low 3 to 3½ hours or until macaroni is almost tender.

2. Stir in salad shrimp and blue cheese; cook, covered, 30-35 minutes longer or until heated through. Just before serving, stir in the chives, parsley and, if desired, additional hot sauce.

DID YOU KNOW?

Cayenne and Tabasco peppers are used in commonly known hot pepper sauces. Tabasco pepper-based sauces are more peppery, while Cayenne pepper-based sauces are milder. Louisiana-style hot sauce is a mild type. With the increased interest in hot sauces in recent years, it's easier than ever to find fiery specialty sauces that are made with hotter peppers.

Slow Cooker Red Beans & Sausage

A native of Louisiana, I like to indulge in my favorite comfort food—red beans. A nice pot of them for Sunday dinner is a tradition that goes back generations in my family. Dig in with some hot buttered corn bread.

—LISA BOWIE LAS VEGAS, NV

PREP: 30 MIN. • **COOK:** 8 HOURS
MAKES: 8 SERVINGS (2¾ QUARTS)

- 1 pound dried red beans
- 1 tablespoon olive oil
- 1 pound fully cooked andouille sausage links, cut into ¼-inch slices
- 1 large onion, chopped
- 1 medium green pepper, chopped
- 2 celery ribs, finely chopped
- 3 teaspoons garlic powder
- 3 teaspoons Creole seasoning
- 2 teaspoons smoked paprika
- 2 teaspoons dried thyme
- 1½ teaspoons pepper
- 6 cups chicken broth
  Hot cooked rice

1. Rinse and sort the red beans; soak according to the package directions.

2. In a large skillet, heat the olive oil over medium-high heat. Brown the andouille sausage. Remove with a slotted spoon. Add the onion, green pepper and celery to skillet; cook and stir 5-6 minutes or until crisp-tender.

3. In a 5- or 6-qt. slow cooker, combine the red beans, sausage, vegetables and seasonings. Stir in the chicken broth. Cook, covered, on low 8-10 hours or until beans are tender.

4. Remove 2 cups of the bean mixture to a bowl. Mash gently with a potato masher. Return to slow cooker; heat through. Serve with rice.

NOTE The following spices may be substituted for 3 teaspoons Creole seasoning: ¾ teaspoon each salt, garlic powder and paprika; and ⅛ teaspoon each dried thyme, ground cumin and cayenne pepper.

Slow Cooker Ham & Eggs, p. 199

CHAPTER 8

BREAKFAST & BRUNCH

Rise and shine with any of these start-your-day sensations.

Brunch Burritos

My cheesy egg burritos stuffed with hash browns, sausage and bacon make a hearty starting point. Everyone builds from there by piling on toppings like jalapenos, hot sauce and salsa.
—**BETH OSBURN** LEVELLAND, TX

PREP: 30 MIN. • **COOK:** 4 HOURS
MAKES: 10 SERVINGS

- 1 pound bulk pork sausage, cooked and drained
- 1/2 pound bacon strips, cooked and crumbled
- 18 eggs, lightly beaten
- 2 cups frozen shredded hash brown potatoes, thawed
- 1 large onion, chopped
- 1 can (10¾ ounces) condensed cheddar cheese soup, undiluted
- 1 can (4 ounces) chopped green chilies
- 1 teaspoon garlic powder
- 1/2 teaspoon pepper
- 2 cups (8 ounces) shredded cheddar cheese
- 10 flour tortillas (10 inches), warmed
  Optional toppings: jalapeno peppers, salsa or hot pepper sauce

1. In a large bowl, combine the first nine ingredients. Pour half of the egg mixture into a 4- or 5-qt. slow cooker coated with cooking spray. Top with half of the shredded cheddar cheese. Repeat layers.

2. Cook, covered, on low 4-5 hours or until the center is set and a thermometer reads 160°.

3. Spoon ¾ cup egg mixture across center of each tortilla. Fold bottom and sides of tortilla over filling and roll up. Add toppings of your choice.

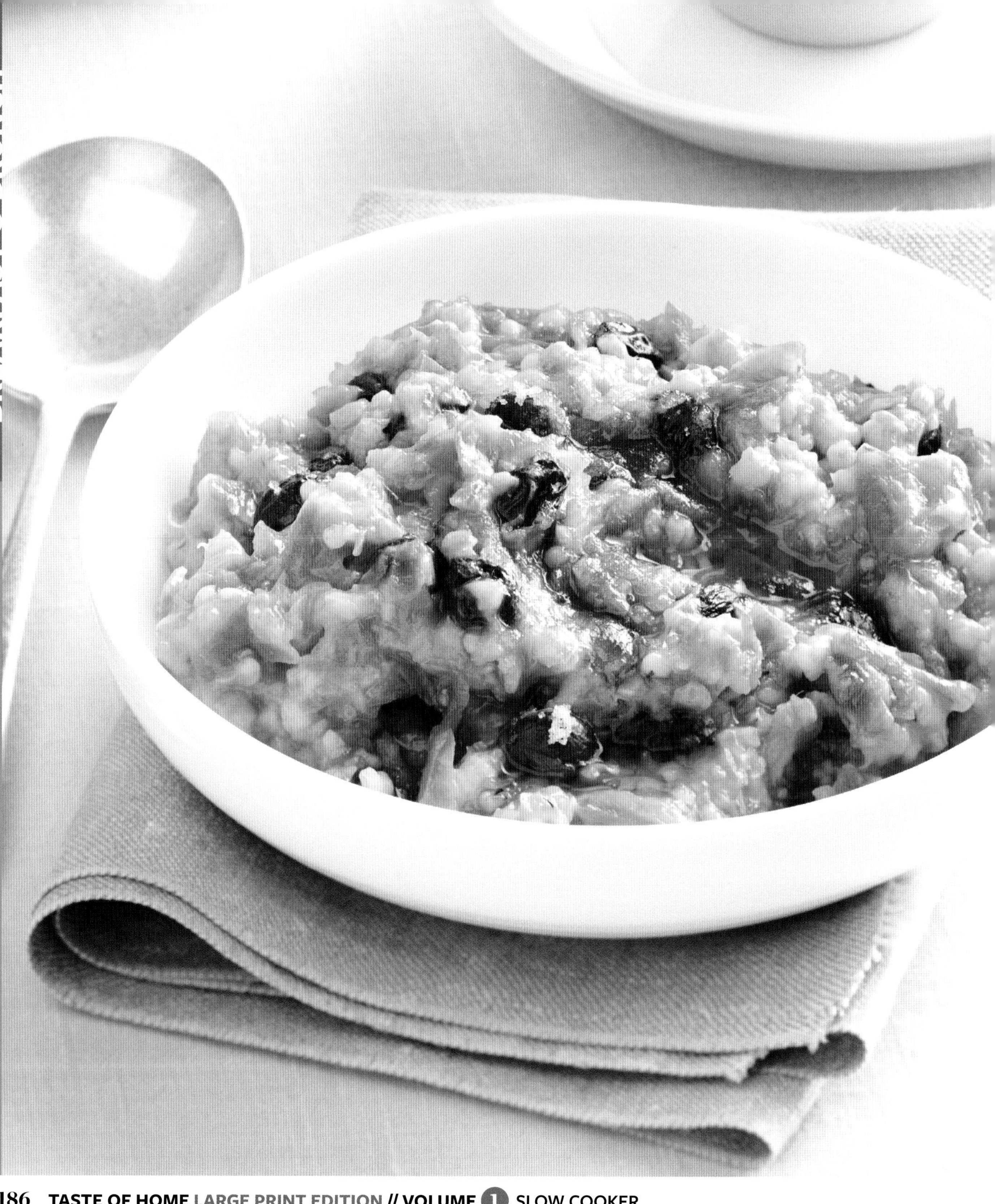

Carrot Cake Oatmeal

Mmm—eating this cereal is like having dessert for breakfast! I love the fact that I can put everything in the slow cooker the night before and wake up in the morning to a wholesome treat. If you like, sprinkle each bowlful with brown sugar or add extra crunch with a garnish of ground nuts.

—DEBBIE KAIN COLORADO SPRINGS, CO

PREP: 10 MIN. • **COOK:** 6 HOURS
MAKES: 8 SERVINGS

4½ cups water
1   can (20 ounces) crushed pineapple, undrained
2   cups shredded carrots
1   cup steel-cut oats
1   cup raisins
2   teaspoons ground cinnamon
1   teaspoon pumpkin pie spice
    Brown sugar, optional

In a 4-qt. slow cooker coated with cooking spray, combine the first seven ingredients. Cover; cook on low for 6-8 hours or until the oats are tender and the liquid is absorbed. Sprinkle with brown sugar if desired.

Chili & Cheese Crustless Quiche

This spicy Tex-Mex quiche is great not only for breakfast, but also for lunch or dinner. Add a simple green salad on the side.
—**GAIL WATKINS** NORWALK, CA

PREP: 15 MIN.
COOK: 3 HOURS + STANDING
MAKES: 6 SERVINGS

- 3 corn tortillas (6 inches)
- 2 cans (4 ounces each) whole green chilies
- 1 can (15 ounces) chili con carne
- 1½ cups (6 ounces) shredded cheddar cheese, divided
- 4 eggs
- 1½ cups 2% milk
- 1 cup biscuit/baking mix
- ¼ teaspoon salt
- ¼ teaspoon pepper
- 1 teaspoon hot pepper sauce, optional
- 1 can (4 ounces) chopped green chilies
- 2 medium tomatoes, sliced
  Sour cream, optional

1. In a greased 4- or 5-qt. slow cooker, layer tortillas, whole green chilies, chili con carne and 1 cup cheddar cheese.

2. In a small bowl, whisk the eggs, milk, biscuit mix, salt, pepper and, if desired, hot pepper sauce until blended; pour into the slow cooker. Top with chopped green chilies and tomatoes.

3. Cook, covered, on low 3-4 hours or until a thermometer reads 160°, sprinkling with remaining cheddar cheese during the last 30 minutes of cooking. Turn off the slow cooker; remove insert. Let quiche stand 15 minutes before serving. If desired, top with sour cream.

TOP TIP

Properly refrigerated, eggs will keep without a significant reduction in quality about 3 weeks after you bring them home. You can check the freshness of an uncooked egg by placing it in a glass of cold water. If the egg is fresh, it will remain on the bottom of the glass.

Hash Brown Egg Breakfast

Expecting company for brunch? Start this all-in-one egg dish cooking earlier in the morning, and you'll have a guaranteed crowd-pleaser to serve guests. Don't be surprised if you see them going back for a second scoop.

—NANCY MARION FROSTPROOF, FL

PREP: 15 MIN. • **COOK:** 3½ HOURS
MAKES: 12 SERVINGS (1⅓ CUPS EACH)

- 1 package (32 ounces) frozen cubed hash brown potatoes, thawed
- 2 cups cubed fully cooked ham
- 1½ cups (6 ounces) shredded cheddar cheese
- 1 large green pepper, chopped
- 1 medium onion, chopped
- 12 eggs, lightly beaten
- 1 cup 2% milk
- 1 teaspoon salt
- 1 teaspoon pepper

1. Layer a third of the potatoes, ham, cheddar cheese, green pepper and onion in a greased 6-qt. slow cooker. Repeat layers twice.

2. In a large bowl, whisk the eggs, milk, salt and pepper; pour over top. Cover and cook on high for 30 minutes. Reduce heat to low; cook for 2½ to 3½ hours or until a thermometer reads 160°.

Hash Browns with Ham

Creamy hash browns with chunks of ham and cheese go over big with just about everyone. I take advantage of convenience products like frozen cubed potatoes and canned cream soup to really speed along the preparation.

—LIGHTNINGBUG *TASTE OF HOME* ONLINE COMMUNITY

PREP: 15 MIN. • **COOK:** 3¼ HOURS
MAKES: 8 SERVINGS

1 package (32 ounces) frozen cubed hash brown potatoes, thawed
1 cup cubed fully cooked ham
1 small onion, chopped
2 cups (8 ounces) shredded cheddar cheese, divided
1 can (14¾ ounces) condensed cream of chicken soup, undiluted
½ cup butter, melted
1 cup (8 ounces) sour cream

1. In a 3-qt. slow cooker, combine hash brown potatoes, ham, onion and 1 cup cheese. Combine soup and butter; pour over the potato mixture. Cover and cook on low for 3-4 hours or until potatoes are tender.

2. Stir in the sour cream. Sprinkle with remaining cheese. Cover and cook for 15 minutes or until cheese is melted.

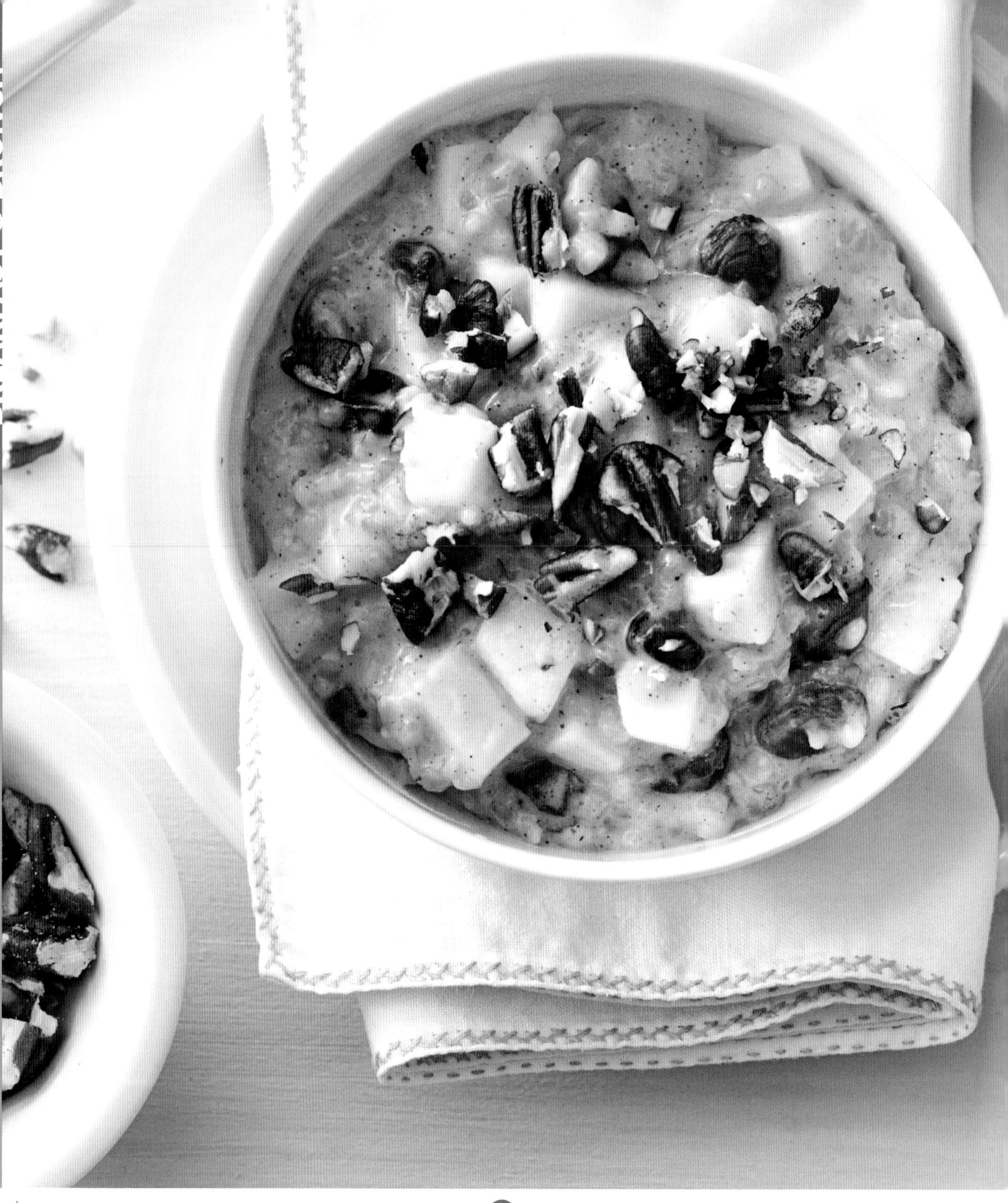

Raisin Nut Oatmeal

Wake up your family in a delightful way with hot, ready-to-eat oatmeal. Full of apple chunks, raisins, cinnamon and pecans, it's sure to start off their day with a smile.

—VALERIE SAUBER ADELANTO, CA

PREP: 10 MIN. • **COOK:** 7 HOURS
MAKES: 6 SERVINGS

3½ cups fat-free milk
  1 large apple, peeled and chopped
  ¾ cup steel-cut oats
  ¾ cup raisins
  3 tablespoons brown sugar
4½ teaspoons butter, melted
  ¾ teaspoon ground cinnamon
  ½ teaspoon salt
  ¼ cup chopped pecans

In a 3-qt. slow cooker coated with cooking spray, combine the first eight ingredients. Cover; cook on low for 7-8 hours or until the liquid is absorbed. Spoon oatmeal into bowls; sprinkle with pecans.

NOTE You may substitute 1½ cups quick-cooking oats for the steel-cut oats and increase the fat-free milk to 4½ cups.

Slow Cooker Breakfast Casserole

Green chilies bring a little extra zip to this satisfying casserole loaded with hash browns, savory sausage and cheddar cheese. I've relied on this dish not only while hosting weekend guests at home, but also while out camping.
—**ELLA STUTHEIT** LAS VEGAS, NV

PREP: 25 MIN. • **COOK:** 7 HOURS
MAKES: 12 SERVINGS

- 1 package (30 ounces) frozen shredded hash brown potatoes
- 1 pound bulk pork sausage, cooked and drained
- 1 medium onion, chopped
- 1 can (4 ounces) chopped green chilies
- 1½ cups (6 ounces) shredded cheddar cheese
- 12 eggs
- 1 cup 2% milk
- ½ teaspoon salt
- ½ teaspoon pepper

In a greased 5- or 6-qt. slow cooker, layer half of the hash brown potatoes, sausage, onion, green chilies and cheese. Repeat layers. In a large bowl, whisk the eggs, milk, salt and pepper; pour over the top. Cover and cook on low for 7-9 hours or until the eggs are set.

Slow Cooker Ham & Eggs

What a fun way to have your eggs! I love serving these neat little wedges, especially on a holiday morning. The minimal prep work means I can spend less time in the kitchen making breakfast and more time with my family.

—ANDREA SCHAAK JORDAN, MN

PREP: 15 MIN. • **COOK:** 3 HOURS
MAKES: 6 SERVINGS

 6 eggs
 1 cup biscuit/baking mix
 ⅔ cup 2% milk
 ⅓ cup sour cream
 2 tablespoons minced fresh parsley
 2 garlic cloves, minced
 ½ teaspoon salt
 ½ teaspoon pepper
 1 cup cubed fully cooked ham
 1 cup (4 ounces) shredded Swiss cheese
 1 small onion, finely chopped
 ⅓ cup shredded Parmesan cheese

1. In a large bowl, whisk the first eight ingredients until blended; stir in remaining ingredients. Pour into a greased 3- or 4-qt. slow cooker.

2. Cook, covered, on low 3-4 hours or until eggs are set. Cut into wedges.

POTLUCK

Slow Cooker Honey Granola

It's so easy to prepare this homemade granola. You may never want to buy the ready-made kind again! Feel free to change up the fruits to suit your preference or the season.
—**ARISA CUPP** WARREN, OR

PREP: 10 MIN. • **COOK:** 2 HOURS + COOLING
MAKES: ABOUT 8 CUPS

- 4 cups old-fashioned oats
- 1 cup sunflower kernels
- 1 cup flaked coconut
- ½ teaspoon salt
- ½ cup canola oil
- ½ cup honey
- 1 cup chopped dried pineapple
- 1 cup chopped dried mangoes

1. In a 3-qt. slow cooker, combine the oats, sunflower kernels, coconut and salt. In a small bowl, whisk the canola oil and honey until blended. Stir into the oats mixture. Cook, covered, on high 2 hours, stirring well every 20 minutes.

2. Remove the granola to baking sheets, spreading evenly; cool completely. Stir in the dried pineapple and mangoes. Store in airtight containers.

Hot Fruit Salad

I let my old-fashioned salad simmer away in the slow cooker while my oven and stovetop are occupied with other dishes. Featuring readily available canned and dried fruits, the tangy medley is a wonderful choice any time of year.

—DEBBIE KIMBROUGH LEXINGTON, MS

PREP: 10 MIN. • **COOK:** 2 HOURS
MAKES: 10 SERVINGS

¾ cup sugar
½ cup butter, melted
¼ teaspoon ground cinnamon
¼ teaspoon ground nutmeg
⅛ teaspoon salt
2 cans (15¼ ounces each) sliced peaches, drained
2 cans (15¼ ounces each) sliced pears, undrained
1 jar (23 ounces) chunky applesauce
½ cup dried apricots, chopped
¼ cup dried cranberries

In a 3-qt. slow cooker, combine sugar, butter, cinnamon, nutmeg and salt. Stir in the remaining ingredients. Cover and cook on high for 2 hours or until heated through.

TOP TIP

Hot Fruit Salad could also make a delicious side dish paired with roasted meat for dinner. Or spoon the warm fruit over slices of purchased pound cake for a fuss-free dessert.

Warm Rocky Road Cake, p. 226

CHAPTER 9

DESSERTS

These tempting sweets make slow cooking a treat.

Caramel Apple Fondue

We indulge in this warm caramel dip on Sunday afternoons in fall when we're watching football on TV. Apple slices make the perfect dippers for the luscious homemade fondue.
—**KATIE KOZIOLEK** HARTLAND, MN

START TO FINISH: 25 MIN.
MAKES: 3½ CUPS

½	cup butter, cubed
2	cups packed brown sugar
1	can (14 ounces) sweetened condensed milk
1	cup light corn syrup
2	tablespoons water
1	teaspoon vanilla extract
	Apple slices

1. In a heavy 3-qt. saucepan, combine the butter, brown sugar, sweetened condensed milk, light corn syrup and water; bring to a boil over medium heat. Cook and stir until a candy thermometer reads 230° (thread stage), about 8-10 minutes. Remove from heat; stir in vanilla.

2. Transfer to a 1½-qt. slow cooker or small fondue pot; keep warm. Serve with apple slices.

NOTE We recommend that you test your candy thermometer before each use by bringing water to a boil; the thermometer should read 212°. Adjust your recipe temperature up or down based on your test.

Very Vanilla Slow Cooker Cheesecake

Slow-cooked cheesecake? Yes! This mini dessert is silky smooth, rich and delicious.
—**KRISTA LANPHIER** MILWAUKEE, WI

PREP: 40 MIN. • **COOK:** 2 HOURS + CHILLING
MAKES: 6 SERVINGS

¾ cup graham cracker crumbs
1 tablespoon sugar plus ⅔ cup sugar, divided
¼ teaspoon ground cinnamon
2½ tablespoons butter, melted
2 packages (8 ounces each) cream cheese, softened
½ cup sour cream
2 to 3 teaspoons vanilla extract
2 eggs, lightly beaten

TOPPING
2 ounces semisweet chocolate, chopped
1 teaspoon shortening
   Toasted sliced almonds

1. Grease a 6-in. springform pan; place on a double thickness of heavy-duty foil (about 12 in. square). Wrap foil securely around pan.

2. Pour 1 in. water into a 6-qt. slow cooker. Layer two 24-in. pieces of aluminum foil. Starting with a long side, roll up the foil to make a 1-in.-wide strip; shape the strip into a circle. Place in the bottom of slow cooker to make a rack.

3. In a small bowl, mix cracker crumbs, 1 tablespoon sugar and cinnamon; stir in butter. Press onto bottom and about 1 in. up sides of prepared pan.

4. In a large bowl, beat cream cheese and remaining sugar until smooth. Beat in sour cream and vanilla. Add eggs; beat on low speed just until combined. Pour into crust.

5. Place the springform pan on foil circle without touching slow cooker sides. Cover slow cooker with a double layer of white paper towels; place the lid securely over towels. Cook, covered, on high 2 hours.

6. Do not remove lid; turn off slow cooker and let cheesecake stand, covered, in slow cooker 1 hour.

7. Remove the springform pan from slow cooker; remove the foil around pan. Cool cheesecake on a wire rack 1 hour longer. Loosen the sides from pan with a knife. Refrigerate overnight, covering when completely cooled.

8. For the topping, in a microwave, melt the chocolate and shortening; stir until smooth. Cool slightly. Remove rim from springform pan. Pour chocolate mixture over cheesecake; sprinkle with almonds.

Classic Bananas Foster

The traditional recipe for this dessert classic makes bananas decadent with caramel sauce, cinnamon and rum. I sprinkle on crunchy walnuts and chewy coconut for good measure.

—CRYSTAL BRUNS ILIFF, CO

PREP: 10 MIN. • **COOK:** 2 HOURS
MAKES: 5 SERVINGS

  5   medium firm bananas
  1   cup packed brown sugar
  ¼   cup butter, melted
  ¼   cup rum
  1   teaspoon vanilla extract
  ½   teaspoon ground cinnamon
  ⅓   cup chopped walnuts
  ⅓   cup flaked coconut
      Vanilla ice cream or sliced pound cake

1. Cut the bananas in half lengthwise, then widthwise; layer in the bottom of a 1½-qt. slow cooker. Combine brown sugar, butter, rum, vanilla and cinnamon; pour over the bananas. Cover and cook on low for 1½ hours or until heated through.

2. Sprinkle with walnuts and coconut; cook 30 minutes longer. Serve with ice cream or pound cake.

Crunchy Candy Clusters

Before I retired, I used to bring my peanut butter clusters to work whenever we were celebrating a special occasion. I still make the crunchy candies during the holiday season because my family loves them. It's hard to eat just one!

—**FAYE O'BRYAN** OWENSBORO, KY

PREP: 15 MIN. • **COOK:** 1 HOUR
MAKES: 6½ DOZEN

  2 pounds white candy coating, coarsely chopped
1½ cups peanut butter
  ½ teaspoon almond extract, optional
  4 cups Cap'n Crunch cereal
  4 cups crisp rice cereal
  4 cups miniature marshmallows

1. Place the white candy coating in a 5-qt. slow cooker. Cover and cook on high for 1 hour. Add the peanut butter. Stir in extract if desired.

2. In a large bowl, combine the cereals and marshmallows. Stir in the peanut butter mixture until well coated. Drop by tablespoonfuls onto waxed paper. Let stand until set. Store at room temperature.

Glazed Cinnamon Apples

Want something sweet but crave comfort food, too? Look no further! These sugar-and-spice apple wedges come out of the slow cooker warm, tender and wonderful.

—**MEGAN MAZE** OAK CREEK, WI

PREP: 20 MIN. • **COOK:** 3 HOURS
MAKES: 7 SERVINGS

6	large tart apples
2	tablespoons lemon juice
½	cup packed brown sugar
½	cup sugar
2	tablespoons all-purpose flour
1	teaspoon ground cinnamon
¼	teaspoon ground nutmeg
6	tablespoons butter, melted
	Vanilla ice cream

1. Peel, core and cut each apple into eight wedges; transfer to a 3-qt. slow cooker. Drizzle with lemon juice. Combine the sugars, flour, cinnamon and nutmeg; sprinkle over the apples. Drizzle with butter.

2. Cover and cook on low for 3-4 hours or until the apples are tender. Serve in dessert dishes with ice cream.

Pumpkin Pie Pudding

My husband loves just about any recipe that has pumpkin in it. He's such a fan of this fall-flavored pudding, I fix it year-round. A dollop of whipped topping and a sprinkling of cinnamon or nutmeg are the perfect finishing touches.
—**ANDREA SCHAAK** BLOOMINGTON, MN

PREP: 10 MIN. • **COOK:** 6 HOURS
MAKES: 6 SERVINGS

- 1 can (15 ounces) solid-pack pumpkin
- 1 can (12 ounces) evaporated milk
- ¾ cup sugar
- ½ cup biscuit/baking mix
- 2 eggs, beaten
- 2 tablespoons butter, melted
- 2½ teaspoons pumpkin pie spice
- 2 teaspoons vanilla extract
  Whipped topping, optional

1. In a large bowl, combine the first eight ingredients. Transfer to a 3-qt. slow cooker coated with cooking spray.

2. Cover; cook on low for 6-7 hours or until a thermometer reads 160°. Serve pudding in bowls with whipped topping if desired.

TOP TIP

If you rarely use pumpkin pie spice in your cooking, you may want to make your own instead of buying it. Combine 4 teaspoons ground cinnamon, 2 teaspoons ground ginger, 1 teaspoon ground cloves and ½ teaspoon ground nutmeg. Store homemade pumpkin pie spice in an airtight container. Yield: 7½ teaspoons.

Strawberry Rhubarb Sauce

Wondering what to do with your homegrown crop of rhubarb? Put it to scrumptious use in a tangy fruit sauce. The rosy topping is especially popular when I spoon it over pound cake, angel food cake or scoops of vanilla ice cream.

—JUDITH WASMAN HARKERS ISLAND, NC

PREP: 10 MIN. • **COOK:** 6 HOURS
MAKES: 10 SERVINGS

- 6 cups chopped rhubarb (½-inch pieces)
- 1 cup sugar
- ½ teaspoon grated orange peel
- ½ teaspoon ground ginger
- 1 cinnamon stick (3 inches)
- ½ cup white grape juice
- 2 cups halved unsweetened strawberries
  Angel food cake, pound cake or vanilla ice cream

1. Place the rhubarb in a 3-qt. slow cooker. Combine sugar, orange peel and ginger; sprinkle over the rhubarb. Add the cinnamon stick and grape juice. Cover and cook on low for 5-6 hours or until rhubarb is tender.

2. Stir in the strawberries; cook 1 hour longer. Discard the cinnamon stick. Serve with cake or ice cream.

Amaretto Cherries with Dumplings

When it comes to dessert, it's hard to beat the tongue-tingling combination of almond flavor with tart cherries. Add a topping of fluffy made-from-scratch dumplings, and you have a bowl of pure bliss.

—TASTE OF HOME TEST KITCHEN

PREP: 15 MIN. • **COOK:** 7¾ HOURS
MAKES: 6 SERVINGS

- 2 cans (14½ ounces each) pitted tart cherries
- ¾ cup sugar
- ¼ cup cornstarch
- ⅛ teaspoon salt
- ¼ cup amaretto or ½ teaspoon almond extract

DUMPLINGS

- 1 cup all-purpose flour
- ¼ cup sugar
- 1 teaspoon baking powder
- ½ teaspoon grated lemon peel
- ⅛ teaspoon salt
- ⅓ cup 2% milk
- 3 tablespoons butter, melted
  Vanilla ice cream, optional

1. Drain cherries, reserving ¼ cup juice. Place cherries in a 3-qt. slow cooker.

2. In a small bowl, mix sugar, cornstarch and salt; stir in the reserved juice until smooth. Stir into cherries. Cook, covered, on high 7 hours. Drizzle amaretto over cherry mixture.

3. For dumplings, in a small bowl, whisk flour, sugar, baking powder, lemon peel and salt. In another bowl, whisk milk and melted butter. Add to flour mixture; stir just until moistened.

4. Drop by tablespoonfuls on top of the hot cherry mixture. Cook, covered, 45 minutes or until a toothpick inserted in center of dumplings comes out clean. If desired, serve warm with ice cream.

TOP TIP

Want to convert a recipe for the slow cooker? Before doing so, check the manufacturer's guidelines for your particular slow cooker. Look for a recipe that is similar to the one you want to convert and use it as a guide.

Blueberry Cobbler

A four-ingredient cobbler that I can get in the slow cooker in 10 minutes—dessert doesn't get much easier than that! I just combine blueberry pie filling, cake mix, pecans and butter. If you prefer, use apple or cherry pie filling instead.
—NELDA CRONBAUGH BELLE PLAINE, IA

PREP: 10 MIN. • **COOK:** 3 HOURS
MAKES: 6 SERVINGS

- 1   can (21 ounces) blueberry pie filling
- 1   package (9 ounces) yellow cake mix
- ¼   cup chopped pecans
- ¼   cup butter, melted
      Vanilla ice cream, optional

Place the blueberry pie filling in a greased 1½-qt. slow cooker. Sprinkle with the yellow cake mix and pecans. Drizzle with butter. Cover and cook on high for 3 hours or until the topping is golden brown. Serve warm with vanilla ice cream if desired.

TOP TIP

Having a party? Make serving ice cream easier. Before guests arrive, scoop the ice cream into cupcake liners, place them on a baking sheet and return them to the freezer until serving time. You won't have to scoop while guests wait—just remove the cupcake liner from each scoop and serve.

Butterscotch-Pecan Bread Pudding

What a way to use day-old bread! Your family and friends are sure to gobble up every last spoonful of this rich, luscious treat. Butterscotch chips, ice cream topping and crunchy chopped pecans give this special pudding its irresistible flavor.
—**LISA VARNER** EL PASO, TX

PREP: 15 MIN. • **COOK:** 3 HOURS
MAKES: 8 SERVINGS

 9 cups cubed day-old white bread (about 8 slices)
 ½ cup chopped pecans
 ½ cup butterscotch chips
 4 eggs
 2 cups half-and-half cream
 ½ cup packed brown sugar
 ½ cup butter, melted
 1 teaspoon vanilla extract
   Whipped cream and butterscotch ice cream topping

1. Place the cubed bread, pecans and butterscotch chips in a greased 4-qt. slow cooker. In a large bowl, whisk the eggs, half-and-half cream, brown sugar, melted butter and vanilla until blended. Pour over the bread mixture; stir gently to combine.

2. Cook, covered, on low 3-4 hours or until a knife inserted in the center comes out clean. Serve warm with whipped cream and butterscotch topping.

Warm Rocky Road Cake

Fresh from the slow cooker, this reminds me of super-moist lava cake. I always keep this recipe handy because it's a real winner.

—SCARLETT ELROD NEWNAN, GA

PREP: 20 MIN. • **COOK:** 3 HOURS
MAKES: 16 SERVINGS

---

1   package German chocolate cake mix (regular size)
1   package (3.9 ounces) instant chocolate pudding mix
1   cup (8 ounces) sour cream
⅓   cup butter, melted
3   eggs
1   teaspoon vanilla extract
3¼ cups 2% milk, divided
1   package (3.4 ounces) cook-and-serve chocolate pudding mix
1½ cups miniature marshmallows
1   cup (6 ounces) semisweet chocolate chips
½   cup chopped pecans, toasted
    Vanilla ice cream, optional

1. In a large bowl, combine the first six ingredients; add 1¼ cups milk. Beat on low speed 30 seconds. Beat on medium 2 minutes. Transfer to a greased 4- or 5-qt. slow cooker. Sprinkle cook-and-serve pudding mix over batter.

2. In a small saucepan, heat remaining milk until bubbles form around sides of pan; gradually pour over dry pudding mix.

3. Cook, covered, on high 3-4 hours or until a toothpick inserted in cake portion comes out with moist crumbs.

4. Turn off the slow cooker. Sprinkle the marshmallows, chocolate chips and pecans over the cake; let stand, covered, 5 minutes or until marshmallows begin to melt. Serve warm. If desired, top with vanilla ice cream.

NOTE To toast nuts, bake in a shallow pan in a 350° oven for 5-10 minutes or cook in a skillet over low heat until lightly browned, stirring occasionally.

Fresh Pumpkin Soup, p. 241

CHAPTER 10

LIGHTER FARE

Choose from slimmed-down recipes that include nutrition facts.

Caramel-Pecan Stuffed Apples

If you crave caramel apples, this lower-calorie version will satisfy your sweet tooth. Cinnamon and nutmeg give the tender fruit a little spice, while pecans add a nice crunch.

—PAM KAISER MANSFIELD, MO

PREP: 20 MIN. • **COOK:** 3 HOURS
MAKES: 6 SERVINGS

- 6 large tart apples
- 2 teaspoons lemon juice
- 1/3 cup chopped pecans
- 1/4 cup chopped dried apricots
- 1/4 cup packed brown sugar
- 3 tablespoons butter, melted
- 3/4 teaspoon ground cinnamon
- 1/4 teaspoon ground nutmeg
  Granola and caramel ice cream topping, optional

1. Core the apples and peel top third of each; brush peeled portions with lemon juice. Place in a 6-qt. slow cooker.

2. Combine pecans, dried apricots, brown sugar, butter, cinnamon and nutmeg. Place a heaping tablespoonful of mixture in each apple. Pour 2 cups water around apples.

3. Cover and cook on low for 3-4 hours or until apples are tender. Serve with granola and caramel topping if desired.

PER SERVING 256 cal., 11 g fat (4 g sat. fat), 15 mg chol., 50 mg sodium, 43 g carb., 6 g fiber, 1 g pro.

Cherry & Spice Rice Pudding

I live in Traverse City, called the "Cherry Capital of the World."
What better way to celebrate our orchards than by using the
fruit in recipes? Here's a comforting treat I love.
—**DEB PERRY** TRAVERSE CITY, MI

PREP: 10 MIN. • **COOK:** 2 HOURS
MAKES: 12 SERVINGS

4 cups cooked long grain rice
1 can (12 ounces) evaporated milk
1 cup 2% milk
1/3 cup sugar
1/4 cup water
3/4 cup dried cherries
3 tablespoons butter, softened
2 teaspoons vanilla extract
1/2 teaspoon ground cinnamon
1/4 teaspoon ground nutmeg

1. In a large bowl, combine the rice, evaporated milk, milk,
sugar and water. Stir in remaining ingredients. Transfer
to a 3-qt. slow cooker coated with cooking spray.

2. Cover and cook on low for 2-3 hours or until the mixture
is thickened. Stir lightly before serving. Serve warm or cold.
Refrigerate leftovers.

PER SERVING 193 cal., 5 g fat (4 g sat. fat), 19 mg chol., 61 mg
sodium, 31 g carb., trace fiber, 4 g pro. **Diabetic Exchanges:**
2 starch, 1 fat.

Cioppino

Looking for fantastic slow-cooked seafood? You've found it! This classic Italian-style fish stew is loaded with clams, crab, haddock and shrimp. Round out your dinner with a fresh green salad or crusty bread.

—LISA MORIARTY WILTON, NH

PREP: 20 MIN. • **COOK:** 4½ HOURS
MAKES: 8 SERVINGS (2½ QUARTS)

- 1 can (28 ounces) diced tomatoes, undrained
- 2 medium onions, chopped
- 3 celery ribs, chopped
- 1 bottle (8 ounces) clam juice
- 1 can (6 ounces) tomato paste
- ½ cup white wine or vegetable broth
- 5 garlic cloves, minced
- 1 tablespoon red wine vinegar
- 1 tablespoon olive oil
- 1 to 2 teaspoons Italian seasoning
- ½ teaspoon sugar
- 1 bay leaf
- 1 pound haddock fillets, cut into 1-inch pieces
- 1 pound uncooked small shrimp, peeled and deveined
- 1 can (6 ounces) lump crabmeat, drained
- 1 can (6 ounces) chopped clams
- 2 tablespoons minced fresh parsley or 2 teaspoons dried parsley flakes

In a 4- or 5-qt. slow cooker, combine the first twelve ingredients. Cover and cook on low for 4-5 hours. Stir in the haddock, shrimp, crabmeat and clams. Cover and cook 30 minutes longer or until the fish flakes easily with a fork and shrimp turn pink. Stir in parsley. Discard bay leaf.

PER SERVING 205 cal., 3 g fat (1 g sat. fat), 125 mg chol., 483 mg sodium, 15 g carb., 3 g fiber, 29 g pro. **Diabetic Exchanges:** 3 lean meat, 2 vegetable.

DID YOU KNOW?

Generally, flavored vinegars and wine vinegars are more subtle than white vinegar, which has a strong, sharp taste. Vinegar should be kept in a cool, dark place. Unopened, it will keep indefinitely; once opened, it can be stored for up to 6 months.

Sausage Pasta Stew

I use my slow cooker to whip up a hearty pasta stew. It's packed with turkey sausage, beans and veggies. My family absolutely inhales it without even realizing it's healthy.
—**SARA BOWEN** UPLAND, CA

PREP: 20 MIN. • **COOK:** 7¼ HOURS
MAKES: 8 SERVINGS

1   pound turkey Italian sausage links, casings removed
4   cups water
1   jar (24 ounces) meatless spaghetti sauce
1   can (16 ounces) kidney beans, rinsed and drained
1   medium yellow summer squash, halved lengthwise and cut into 1-inch pieces
2   medium carrots, sliced
1   medium sweet red or green pepper, diced
⅓   cup chopped onion
1½ cups uncooked spiral pasta
1   cup frozen peas
1   teaspoon sugar
½   teaspoon salt
¼   teaspoon pepper

1. In a nonstick skillet, cook the sausage over medium heat until no longer pink; drain and place in a 5-qt. slow cooker. Stir in the water, spaghetti sauce, kidney beans, yellow summer squash, carrots, red pepper and onion.

2. Cover and cook on low for 7-9 hours or until vegetables are tender.

3. Stir in the spiral pasta, peas, sugar, salt and pepper. Cover and cook on high for 15-20 minutes or until pasta is tender.

PER SERVING 276 cal., 6 g fat (2 g sat. fat), 30 mg chol., 1,111 mg sodium, 38 g carb., 6 g fiber, 18 g pro. **Diabetic Exchanges:** 1½ starch, 2 lean meat, 2 vegetable.

Fall Garden Medley

The vibrant colors of this dish always make it stand out from the rest. And the taste is even better! Carrots, onions, sweet potatoes and beets add up to a hearty side.

—KRYSTINE KERCHER LINCOLN, NE

PREP: 20 MIN. • **COOK:** 5 HOURS
MAKES: 8 SERVINGS

4 large carrots, cut into 1½-inch pieces
3 fresh beets, peeled and cut into 1½-inch pieces.
2 medium sweet potatoes, peeled and cut into 1½-inch pieces
2 medium onions, peeled and quartered
½ cup water
2 teaspoons salt
½ teaspoon pepper
¼ teaspoon dried thyme
1 tablespoon olive oil
Fresh parsley or dried parsley flakes, optional

1. Place the carrots, beets, sweet potatoes, onions and water in a greased 3-qt. slow cooker. Sprinkle with salt, pepper and thyme. Drizzle with olive oil. Cover and cook on low for 5-6 hours or until tender.

2. Stir the vegetables and sprinkle with parsley if desired.

PER SERVING 83 cal., 2 g fat (trace sat. fat), 0 chol., 633 mg sodium, 16 g carb., 3 g fiber, 2 g pro. **Diabetic Exchanges:** 1 vegetable, ½ starch.

Fresh Pumpkin Soup

Mmm—what a wonderful way to savor fall! Fresh pumpkin, tart apples, chicken broth and just five other ingredients go into the slow cooker. The result is a smooth, savory soup I top off with toasted seeds.

—**JANE SHAPTON** IRVINE, CA

PREP: 50 MIN. • **COOK:** 8 HOURS
MAKES: 9 SERVINGS (ABOUT 2 QUARTS)

- 8 cups chopped fresh pumpkin (about 3 pounds)
- 4 cups chicken broth
- 3 small tart apples, peeled and chopped
- 1 medium onion, chopped
- 2 tablespoons lemon juice
- 2 teaspoons minced fresh gingerroot
- 2 garlic cloves, minced
- ½ teaspoon salt

TOASTED PUMPKIN SEEDS

- ½ cup fresh pumpkin seeds
- 1 teaspoon canola oil
- ⅛ teaspoon salt

1. In a 5-qt. slow cooker, combine the first eight ingredients. Cover and cook on low for 8-10 hours or until the pumpkin and apples are tender.

2. Meanwhile, toss pumpkin seeds with oil and salt. Spread onto an ungreased 15x10x1-in. baking pan. Bake at 250° for 45-50 minutes or until golden brown. Set aside.

3. Cool soup slightly; process in batches in a blender. Transfer to a large saucepan; heat through. Garnish with toasted seeds.

PER SERVING 102 cal., 2 g fat (0.55 g sat. fat), 0 chol., 567 mg sodium, 22 g carb., 3 g fiber, 3 g pro. **Diabetic Exchanges:** 1 starch, ½ fruit.

HOW TO

MAKE A SEED SNACK

To toast pumpkin seeds for snacking, follow the directions here for toasting the seeds, substituting garlic salt for the salt if desired. Let the seeds cool completely and store them in an airtight container for up to 3 weeks.

Slow-Cooked Coconut Chicken

One of the best things about this chicken is how incredible it makes my kitchen smell. Everyone who stops by asks, "What are you cooking?" And anyone who takes a bite wants to go home with the recipe!

—**ANN SMART** NORTH LOGAN, UT

PREP: 10 MIN. • **COOK:** 4 HOURS
MAKES: 6 SERVINGS

½   cup light coconut milk
2   tablespoons brown sugar
2   tablespoons reduced-sodium soy sauce
2   garlic cloves, minced
⅛   teaspoon ground cloves
6   boneless skinless chicken thighs (about 1½ pounds)
6   tablespoons flaked coconut, toasted
    Minced fresh cilantro

In a large bowl, combine the first five ingredients. Place chicken in a 3-qt. slow cooker. Pour coconut milk mixture over the top. Cook, covered, on low 4-5 hours or until the chicken is tender. Serve with coconut and cilantro.

NOTE To toast coconut, bake in a shallow pan in a 350° oven for 5-10 minutes, or cook in a skillet over low heat until golden brown, stirring occasionally.

PER SERVING 201 cal., 10 g fat (3 g sat. fat), 76 mg chol., 267 mg sodium, 6 g carb., trace fiber, 21 g pro. **Diabetic Exchanges:** 3 lean meat, ½ starch, ½ fat.

DID YOU KNOW?

Coconut milk is a sweet milky white liquid, high in oil, derived from the meat of a mature coconut. It is not the naturally occurring liquid found inside a coconut. In the United States, coconut milk is usually sold in cans and used in both savory and sweet dishes originating in tropical or Asian cuisines.

Light Ham Tetrazzini

Creamy, cheesy and loaded with ham, this entree may seem too indulgent to be called "light." But reduced-sodium and reduced-fat ingredients make it a guilt-free hit. Multigrain spaghetti boosts the fiber content, too.
—**SUSAN BLAIR** STERLING, MI

PREP: 15 MIN. • **COOK:** 4 HOURS
MAKES: 10 SERVINGS

2 cans (10¾ ounces each) reduced-fat reduced-sodium condensed cream of mushroom soup, undiluted
2 cups sliced fresh mushrooms
2 cups cubed fully cooked ham
1 cup fat-free evaporated milk
¼ cup white wine or water
2 teaspoons prepared horseradish
1 package (14½ ounces) multigrain spaghetti
1 cup shredded Parmesan cheese

1. In a 5-qt. slow cooker, mix the first six ingredients. Cook, covered, on low 4-5 hours until heated through.

2. Cook the spaghetti according to the package directions; drain. Stir into slow cooker. Add the Parmesan cheese; toss to combine.

PER SERVING 279 cal., 5 g fat (2 g sat. fat), 26 mg chol., 734 mg sodium, 37 g carb., 4 g fiber, 20 g pro. **Diabetic Exchanges:** 2½ starch, 1 lean meat, ½ fat.

Onion-Garlic Hash Browns

Dress up ordinary frozen hash browns with veggies, garlic and seasonings for a flavorful side dish that goes with many main courses. When I want to splurge a little, I sprinkle on some shredded cheddar cheese before serving.

—CINDI BOGER ARDMORE, AL

PREP: 20 MIN. • **COOK:** 3 HOURS
MAKES: 12 SERVINGS (½ CUP EACH)

- 1 large red onion, chopped
- 1 small sweet red pepper, chopped
- 1 small green pepper, chopped
- ¼ cup butter, cubed
- 1 tablespoon olive oil
- 4 garlic cloves, minced
- 1 package (30 ounces) frozen shredded hash brown potatoes
- ½ teaspoon salt
- ½ teaspoon pepper
- 3 drops hot pepper sauce, optional
- 2 teaspoons minced fresh parsley

1. In a large skillet, saute the onion and peppers in butter and oil until crisp-tender. Add the garlic; cook 1 minute longer. Stir in hash browns, salt, pepper and hot pepper sauce if desired.

2. Transfer to a 5-qt. slow cooker coated with cooking spray. Cover; cook on low for 3-4 hours or until heated through. Sprinkle with parsley before serving.

PER SERVING 110 cal., 5 g fat (3 g sat. fat), 10 mg chol., 136 mg sodium, 15 g carb., 1 g fiber, 2 g pro. **Diabetic Exchanges:** 1 starch, 1 fat.

Pepper Steak

Pepper steak is one of my favorite dishes, but I was often disappointed when the beef came out too tough. This recipe solved that problem completely! The slow cooker keeps things simple and makes the meat so tender. I like to store any leftovers we may have in individual portions for quick lunches.

—JULIE RHINE ZELIENOPLE, PA

PREP: 30 MIN. • **COOK:** 6¼ HOURS
MAKES: 12 SERVINGS

1 beef top round roast (3 pounds)
1 large onion, halved and sliced
1 large green pepper, cut into ½-inch strips
1 large sweet red pepper, cut into ½-inch strips
1 cup water
4 garlic cloves, minced
⅓ cup cornstarch
½ cup reduced-sodium soy sauce
2 teaspoons sugar
2 teaspoons ground ginger
8 cups hot cooked brown rice

1. Place the roast, onion and peppers in a 5-qt. slow cooker. Add water and garlic. Cook, covered, on low 6-8 hours or until meat is tender.

2. Remove the beef to a cutting board. Transfer the vegetables and cooking juices to a large saucepan. Bring to a boil. In a small bowl, mix the cornstarch, soy sauce, sugar and ginger until smooth; stir into the vegetable mixture. Return to a boil, stirring constantly; cook and stir 1-2 minutes or until thickened.

3. Cut beef into slices. Stir gently into sauce; heat through. Serve with rice.

FREEZE OPTION Freeze the cooled beef mixture in freezer containers. To use, partially thaw in the refrigerator overnight. Heat through in a saucepan, stirring occasionally and adding a little water if necessary.

PER SERVING 322 cal., 5 g fat (1 g sat. fat), 64 mg chol., 444 mg sodium, 38 g carb., 3 g fiber, 30 g pro. **Diabetic Exchanges:** 3 lean meat, 2 starch.

GENERAL RECIPE INDEX

ALPHABETICAL RECIPE INDEX